Improve Your Communication Skills

CREATING SUCCESS
SERIES

The above titles are available from all good bookshops.

For further information on these and other Kogan Page titles, or to order online, visit www.koganpage.com.

Sixth edition

Improve Your Communication Skills

How to build trust, be heard and communicate with confidence

Alan Barker

KoganPage

Publisher's note

Every possible effort has been made to ensure that the information contained in this book is accurate at the time of going to press, and the publishers and author cannot accept responsibility for any errors or omissions, however caused. No responsibility for loss or damage occasioned to any person acting, or refraining from action, as a result of the material in this publication can be accepted by the editor, the publisher or the author.

First published in Great Britain and the United States in 2008 by Kogan Page Limited
Sixth edition 2022

2nd Floor, 45 Gee Street	8 W 38th Street, Suite 902	4737/23 Ansari Road
London	New York, NY 10018	Daryaganj
EC1V 3RS	USA	New Delhi 110002
United Kingdom		India
www.koganpage.com		

ISBNs

Hardback	9781398605909
Paperback	9781398605824
Ebook	9781398605893

British Library Cataloguing-in-Publication Data
A CIP record for this book is available from the British Library.

Library of Congress Cataloging-in-Publication Control Number
2022937019

Typeset by Hong Kong FIVE Workshop
Print production managed by Jellyfish
Printed and bound by CPI Group (UK) Ltd, Croydon CR0 4YY

CONTENTS

ABOUT THE AUTHORS

We all need to communicate better at work. A survey by the Economist Intelligence Unit (EIU), conducted in 2017 in the US, found that miscommunication is delaying projects and contributing to lost sales, as well as increasing stress and destroying morale.

And the problem is affecting our organizations at every level.

If you're a senior manager, you might see the problem as one of leadership. Two-thirds of business leaders surveyed by the Interact consultancy in 2016 said that 'there is something about their role as a leader that makes them uncomfortable communicating with their employees'.

You may be one of those employees. You might be a millennial, born between 1981 and 1999: one of a generation who generally use social media at work far more than their (mainly) older managers. According to Art Markman, Professor of Psychology and Marketing at the University of Texas at Austin, millennials wishing to become leaders will need to master the skills of communicating in person: 'We have a generation,' he explains in the EIU report, 'who is not as practised at engaging in real time with people.'

If you're a middle manager, you face a particular challenge. You spend a lot of time shuttling information and ideas between senior and junior execs. As Mr Markman explains, 'Communication is one of the most significant parts of [a middle manager's] job because they're dealing with the widest variety of people.'

And if you're entering the world of work, it's worth knowing that communication skills head the list of must-haves in new recruits. In the Graduate Management Admission Council's (GMAC's) 2017 Corporate Recruiters Survey, the two top-rated skills that employers look for when hiring are speaking and listening. Third in line is adaptability, the ability to flex communication style. Written skills and presentation skills take the next two places.

Interestingly, employers rated managerial skills consistently as least important.

The GMAC's survey reflects the fact that every organization is a network of conversations. Our success depends on the way we speak and listen to each other. Most of us know that: 65 per cent of those surveyed in the EIU report rated face-to-face meetings as very effective, but only 22 per cent claimed to have such meetings every day. Globalization, outsourcing and flexible working are making it harder to talk face-to-face. Ever more rigorous auditing forces co-workers sitting at the same desk to exchange emails. We look at screens, some of us, more than we look at each other.

It starts with us. If we can speak and listen more effectively, then our videoconferences, presentations and reports will all improve. More than that, we'll be able to adapt our own communication styles to the increasingly varied styles our colleagues bring to work.

That's why, in this new edition, you'll find a questionnaire to help you identify your own preferred style and become a more adaptable communicator. It's why I've created a new chapter on the skills of storytelling and narrative – skills that are increasingly in demand in organizations of all kinds. And it's why I've maintained a core focus on the four top-rated skills of corporate communication. Speaking, listening, presenting and writing: master those skills and you'll be well placed to win the job you want, manage more efficiently and lead more effectively.

01
What is communication?

Communicate: it's what we humans do. We're not alone, of course: every living thing sends messages in one way or another, to help it navigate its environment or attract others. Movements, sounds, scents – even the shape and colour of a flower communicates useful information to the insects or birds that are drawn to it.

But we humans seem to have developed certain kinds of communication to a rare pitch of sophistication. Our command of spoken language is extraordinary; but just as impressive are our abilities to read facial expressions, tone of voice and gestures.

In fact, communicating comes so naturally to most of us that it's sometimes hard to see why it goes wrong – especially at work. Why should a skill that comes to most of us so effortlessly become such a tortuous process in an organization?

Let's begin by thinking about what we mean by the word 'communication'.

Exercise

Complete this sentence in no more than 12 words.

Communication is...

Ask a few colleagues for their ideas. Compare your thoughts.
Are you defining communication in all its forms? Are you defining effective communication? What makes communication ineffective? Can you agree on a definition?

The transmission model

In the 19th century, the word 'communication' referred mainly to the movement of goods and people. We still use the word like this, of course: roads and railways are forms of communication, just as much as speaking or writing.

And we still use industrial metaphors for communication. Information, like freight, needs to be stored, transferred and retrieved. And we often describe the movement of information in terms of a 'channel', along which information 'flows'.

In the 20th century, this transport metaphor readily adapted itself to new, electronic technologies: we have 'telephone lines' and 'television channels'. Electronic information comes in 'bits', stored in 'files' or 'vaults'. The words 'download' and 'upload' use the freight metaphor; email uses postal imagery.

So it wouldn't be surprising, in that exercise just now, if you defined communication as 'the effective transfer of information'. We 'have' an idea (as if the idea were an object). We 'put the idea into words' (like putting it into a box); we try to 'put our idea across' (by 'conveying' it); and the 'receiver' – hopefully – 'gets' the idea. We may need to 'unpack' the idea before the receiver can fully 'grasp' it. Of course, we need to be careful to avoid 'information overload'.

This is the transmission model of communication. And it's very powerful. It governs all the processes and policies by which we communicate in organizations. It suggests that information is objective and measurable (how many bits are we transmitting?). Above all, the model's simple: we can draw a diagram to illustrate it.

Turning the transmission model around

So what's wrong with the transmission model? Well, to begin with, it doesn't seem to reflect the way people actually communicate.

Wii's laws of communication

Osmo Wii, a Finnish professor, developed these laws of corporate communication. They describe with frightening accuracy the failings of the transmission model, especially in organizations.

- Communication usually fails, except by accident.
- If communication can fail, it will fail.
- If communication cannot fail, it still usually fails.
- If communication seems to succeed in the way you intend – someone's misunderstood.
- If you are content with your message, communication is certainly failing.
- If a message can be interpreted in several ways, it will be interpreted in a manner that maximizes the damage.
- There is always someone who knows better than you what your message means.
- The more we communicate, the more communication fails.

Perhaps the transmission metaphor is inaccurate. After all, a message isn't really like a parcel. When I send the parcel, it's no longer with me; in contrast, when I send a message, I still have it.

But there's a more serious reason why the transmission model fails to describe communication accurately.

The model's the wrong way around.

Here's the first and most important point: communication begins, not with transmission, but with understanding. No matter how effectively I transmit a message, it won't communicate to you if you don't understand it. If we want to improve our communication skills, we could start by focusing, not on how we transmit information and ideas, but on how we *understand* them.

Pattern-matching:
The secret of understanding

So how *do* we understand? The simple answer is: by pattern-matching. Mental models in our brains filter the information we pick up through our five senses and create meaning.

Here's a very simple example. Take a look at Figure 1.1.

Figure 1.1 A Kanizsa triangle

What can you see? Probably a white triangle. Of course, there *is* no white triangle; your brain has matched the available information to its store of mental models, and come up with the best guess of a white triangle. (The triangle's named after Gaetano Kanizsa, an Italian psychologist and artist, founder of the Institute of Psychology of Trieste.)

Scientists call this process of filling in the gaps 'perceptual completion', and it's not limited to visual information. How can I distinguish your voice from all the other noise in a crowded room? How can a taste bring back a childhood memory, or a scent remind us of someone we love? Our brains match information to a mental model and *complete* the pattern. As Stephen Jay Gould famously said: 'The mind, basically, is a pattern-seeking machine.'

Our mental models make sense of the world for us. Indeed, they create the world for us. As Joe Griffin and Ivan Tyrrell explain in their book *Human Givens*, 'without mental models, no world would exist for us. They organize our reality'.

Getting to know each other

Pattern-matching isn't restricted to triangles, tunes and perfumes. Every time we encounter another person, they're pattern-matching, seeking to understand us by using the mental models that they've developed. Those models are considerably more complicated and various than a white triangle; but the *process* of pattern-matching is just the same. And that process is happening, even if we're not trying to communicate. All that's necessary is that someone is observing us.

We can't *not* communicate. Or, to paraphrase Marshall McLuhan: the effect we have on others is what we communicate.

Top tip

Whenever you start a conversation, try to ask yourself: 'What effect am I having here?' And then ask: 'What effect do I *want* to have?'

Pattern-matching is never a one-way process. Just as the other person is seeking to understand us, so we pattern-match to try to understand them. Each of us is noticing each other's words, expressions and behaviour, and making a best guess about the information we're receiving. If we want to continue the process, we'll try to match our patterns *to each other*.

And so begins a subtle dance between us: the gentle exchange of attention and action that we call conversation. We start to mirror each other's stance and each other's gestures; our voices begin to chime together, matching rhythm, pace and pitch. We may even begin to anticipate each other's words and finish each other's sentences.

Building rapport

We usually refer to this process of establishing mutual understanding as 'building rapport'. And the images we use to describe it aren't the images of railways or couriers. We don't talk about transmitting information. Instead, we might use the language of music. You may feel that I'm 'on your wavelength'; I may feel that we're 'in tune'. Perhaps we feel 'a sense of harmony', or that 'we're singing from the same song sheet'. Rapport is one of the great pleasures of human communication, and when it doesn't happen, we can feel uncomfortable or disappointed.

Most rapport occurs spontaneously. But we can build it deliberately. When we do so, rapport becomes more than an enjoyable activity; it becomes a communication skill.

To develop our rapport-building skills, we need to think about our:

- visual behaviour;
- vocal behaviour; and
- verbal behaviour.

Overwhelmingly, we believe what we see. If there's a mismatch between what I say and what my body's doing, you're going to believe my body. So building rapport deliberately must begin with giving the visual signs of being welcoming, relaxed and open. And visual rapport extends to the way we look: our stance, the way we relate to the other person in space, even our clothes.

The music of the voice builds vocal rapport. We can vary our pitch (how high or low the tone of voice is), pace (the speed of speaking) and volume (how loudly or softly we speak). If any of these three elements jars with the other person, they'll feel uncomfortable.

Top tip

Think about developing your vocal skills. Consider joining Toastmasters to practise your public speaking. Joining a choir can work wonders for your voice – and your social skills.

We build verbal rapport through the words we speak. If the other person feels that we're speaking their language, they'll feel more comfortable with us and more willing to continue the conversation. Listen to the words the other person uses and try to use them yourself.

Most of us know what it's like to feel 'lost for words'. How can we start a conversation with someone we don't know well, at a networking event, in a meeting, or in a performance review?

The key is to ask a question. Look for something in your shared situation to talk about, and ask a question relating to that. Avoid talking about yourself, and avoid asking a direct question that the other person might find intrusive. Take the initiative. Put the other person at ease, and you'll soon relax yourself.

Exercise

Here's a simple method to establish rapport with someone you don't know. Try it out in the staff restaurant, at social gatherings, in networking meetings and at conferences.

1   Copy the other person's body language to create a 'mirror image'.

2   Ask three questions – but no more than three until you've done the next two things.

3   Find something from what you've just learned that will allow you to compliment the other person – subtly.

4 Find something in what you have found out to agree with.

5 Repeat steps 1 to 4 until the conversation takes on a life of its own.

(With thanks to Chris Dyas.)

Communication: A new definition

We need, then, to redefine the word 'communication'. The transmission model cannot begin to describe this complex process – pattern-matching, rapport-building, the nuances of conversation – adequately.

The clue to a possible new definition lies in the history of the word. 'Communication' derives from the Latin *communis*, meaning 'shared'. It belongs to the family of words that includes *communion*, *communism* and *community*.

Top tip

Communication is the process of creating shared understanding.

We seek to create shared understanding in all sorts of ways. We speak on the phone and hold videoconferences; we spend hours producing slides for corporate presentations; we write emails and texts, reports, web pages and blog posts.

But we also communicate less formally. We chat and gossip; we tell jokes; perhaps most importantly, we tell each other stories. All of these activities create rapport, build relationships and generate shared understanding – often far more effectively than the more official channels of communication in our organizations.

Conversation: The currency of communication

The basic unit of human communication remains what it has always been: conversation.

We hold conversations to build relationships and to make sense of reality. We influence each other's thoughts, feelings and actions by holding conversations. We converse to solve problems, to co-operate and find new things to do. Conversation is our way of imagining and creating the future.

Every conversation is a dynamic process of listening and speaking. It uses language: words, of course, but also those other kinds of language that we've just mentioned: visual language like gestures and eye contact; and vocal language, expressed in the music of our voices.

We can think of a conversation as being like a verbal dance. The word 'conversation' comes from Latin words meaning 'to move around with'. Different kinds of conversation, like different kinds of dance, have different rules.

Exercise

Think about the words we use to describe different kinds of conversation. Write down a few of them. How do they differ? Can you identify any of the rules that apply to each?

For example, you might think of the word 'chat', and the word 'discussion'. What's the difference between the two? Do chats and discussions follow different rules?

Can you think of any other words describing different kinds of conversation?

As our conversations grow and develop, the skills of listening and speaking become the broader, deeper skills of enquiry, persuasion, explanation and storytelling. In Chapters 4, 5 and 6, we'll explore those four sets of skills. We all balance these skills in different ways. Those differences contribute to our different communication styles – and it's those styles we'll explore in the next chapter.

Summary points

- Communication begins, not with transmission, but with understanding.

- Understanding is a pattern-matching process.

- Sometimes, we have to fill in the gaps to make the pattern.

- By asking: 'What effect am I having?' in any conversation, we can begin to build rapport.

- We can build rapport deliberately, by managing our:

  – physical behaviour;

  – vocal behaviour; and

  – verbal behaviour.

- Communication is the process of creating shared understanding.

- Conversation is the principal tool we use.

02
What's your communication style?

We all communicate in different ways. And that can cause problems. In the 2017 survey conducted by the Economist Intelligence Unit, the most frequently cited cause of poor communication at work was a clash of different communication styles. In the words of the survey's authors, 'managers need to tailor their communication styles to those around them to be effective'.

In this chapter, we'll look at different styles of communicating. We'll discover the style or styles that we prefer; we'll learn how to assess other people's preferences; and, most importantly, we'll discover how to adapt our own style to different situations.

Communication style questionnaire

Take a look at this list of phrases. Decide which of them best describe the way you communicate, and put a ring around the letter beside it. You can mark as many or as few phrases as you wish.

Likes to be in control	f
Prefers a lot of detail on which to base decisions	a
Expresses ideas spontaneously, sometimes without thinking	e
Finds it difficult to say 'no' when asked to do something	s

Neat and organized	a
Looks for firm decisions and clear actions	f
Prefers to be a team player	s
Likes to talk about the 'big picture'	e
Seeks overt approval and praise	e
Dislikes inaction	f
Good at counselling others	s
Likes to base ideas on numbers and statistics	a
Prefers maximum freedom to manage themselves and others	f
Knows where to find the data needed to solve a problem	a
Good at gaining support from others	s
Knows and applies the rules	f
Does things one step at a time	a
Can become impatient with others' feelings, attitudes and advice	f
Searches for a workable compromise	s
Encourages and energizes others	e
Decides and acts cautiously	a
Good at making presentations and speeches	e
Technically proficient	f
Needs others' support to set goals	s
Gets bored with too much talking and too little doing	f
Prepares and studies things in advance	a
Breaks processes into steps and explains each step	f
Uses statistics and evidence to prove arguments	a
Likes to inspire others	e
Wants to keep the peace	s
Good at finding practical solutions to problems	f
Good ice-breaker and socializer	s
Dreams and inspires others to dream	e

Breaks information into parts to understand it	a
Likes making decisions	f
Enjoys variety and change	e
Sensitive to others' feelings	s
Looks for the right way to do something	f
Prefers to work alone on problems	a
Seeks security and a sense of belonging	s
Likes to be asked by others to find the answer	f
Never trusts opinions unsupported by facts	a
Tends to thrive on adrenaline	e
Reads people well	s
Does not like to waste time	f
Thinks best by discussing ideas with other people	e
Needs a conceptual framework to solve problems	a
Dislikes conflict	s

Now count up all the instances of each letter you have ringed. The total is your score for that letter. For example, if you have ringed the letter 'f' six times, your score for 'f' is 6.

Record your score for each letter here:

s:

a:

f:

e:

Now transfer your scores onto Figure 2.1. Mark each score on the appropriate diagonal line: 's' stands for 'Social', 'a' for 'Analytical', 'f' for 'Functional', and 'e' for 'Expressive'. Lower scores sit towards the centre of the diagram, and higher scores toward the edge.

Join each of the four points you have marked with straight lines, to create a four-sided shape. Mark that shape strongly so that you can see your communication style profile clearly.

Figure 2.1 Communication styles map

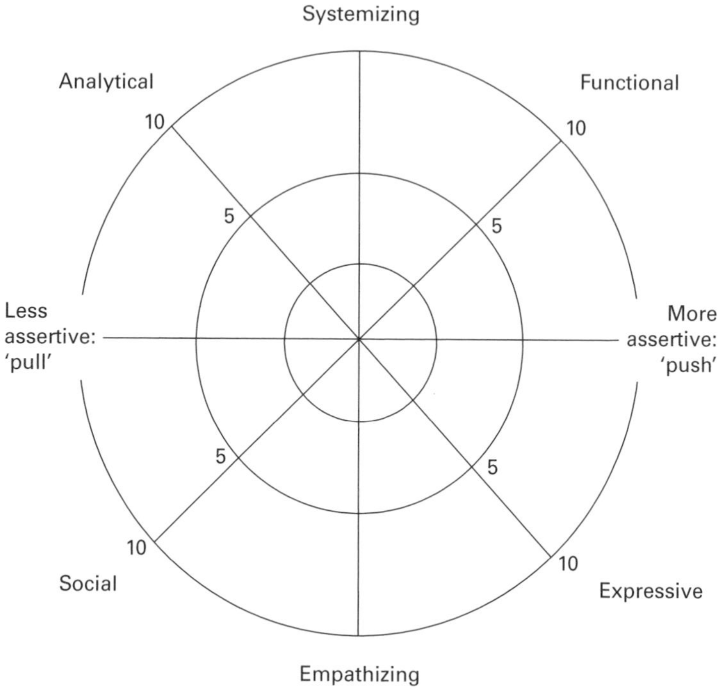

Understanding your communication profile

This communication profile is based on two sets of complementary behaviours. Together, they create a useful picture of the ways we prefer to communicate with others.

Push and pull: Managing status

The first pair of complementary behaviours express our relationship in a conversation.

We can model this relationship using the idea of status. Status is our position relative to each other – and it's brutally simple: by definition, our status can only be higher or lower than that of the person we're communicating with. Think of status as being like a see-saw: if we raise our status, the other person's status automatically goes down. If we raise their status, our end of the see-saw automatically dips. We can think of rapport – which we looked at in the previous chapter – as *levelling* status.

The shorthand for raising our own status is 'pushing'. The core 'push' behaviour is to speak. Examples of 'pushing', in increasing order of intensity, might include making a statement, persuading, bargaining, criticizing, instructing, invoking rules, demanding, or giving orders. Ultimately, of course, 'pushing' involves the use of force.

Conversely, the shorthand for raising the other person's status is 'pulling', and the core 'pull' behaviour is to listen. Other examples, in increasing order of intensity, might include asking a question, exploring an idea, encouraging, praising, giving way, or obeying.

The behaviours of 'pushing' and 'pulling' are on a spectrum. Most conversations will include a mix of both, because most conversations include a mix of speaking and listening. Most of us can do both, and we can develop our skills in both. But most of us will tend to prefer one set of these behaviours over the other: put simply, we tend to prefer either speaking or listening.

Empathizing and systemizing

The second pair of complementary behaviours express how we prefer to understand the world around us.

We saw in the previous chapter that understanding is principally about pattern-matching. We seek to match our experiences with mental models that we've built up in our minds. People with very different mental models will have to work harder to understand each other. What the Economist Intelligence Unit report calls 'a clash of communication styles' is also a clash of mental models.

Empathizing and systemizing are two modes of pattern-matching, and they look at the world in two different ways.

Empathizing is the drive to identify another person's emotions and thoughts, and to respond to them with appropriate behaviour. It arises out of a natural desire to care for others, and an awareness of how others see us. We empathize when we sense that someone's emotions have shifted, and we wonder why. Empathy helps us tune in to another person's world, and pattern-match to their mental models. It stops us offending, insulting or injuring them. Empathizing starts from the understanding that ours may not be the only way to look at the world, and that others' mental models – their thoughts, feelings and values – matter as much as ours.

Top tip

Think about someone with whom you find it hard to empathize. Can you pick out specific ways in which you each see the world differently? If you can identify a particular mental model that this person seems to hold, can you imagine holding that same mental model? How would your view of the world change?

Systemizing is the drive to understand our environment by constructing systems. A system is any set of elements that operates on inputs and delivers outputs, according to 'if-then' rules. If it rains, the pond in the garden fills with water. If I flick the switch, then the light will come on. If I add two to three using the rules of decimal addition, I get five. If sea water rises to a certain temperature, coral reefs will die.

Systemizing seeks to understand how things work, and in particular the *rules* that govern how they work. The great advantage of systemizing is that it allows us to predict how a system will behave. Systemizing gives us control over our environment.

Systems come in all shapes and sizes. According to Simon Baron-Cohen, we can recognize (at least) six types of system: technical (machines of any kind), natural (an organism, a pond, a forest), abstract (languages, computer codes), social (teams, companies, families), organizable (encyclopedias, libraries), and motoric (playing a musical instrument, swimming).

Just as 'pushing' and 'pulling' are on a spectrum, so empathizing and systemizing are complementary processes. We can all – most of us – both empathize and systemize. But we tend to prefer one or the other, and that preference will affect our communication style.

Four communication styles

We can combine these two spectra of behaviour – 'push'/'pull', empathize/systemize – to create four broad styles of communication: Social, Analytical, Functional and Expressive. (The acronym SAFE will help you remember them.) Most of us prefer one or two of these styles over the others. Identifying your own preferred styles will help you extend your skills into other styles – and become a more competent communicator.

A word of caution here. We're talking here about *style*; we're not discussing what kind of person you are. Just as we prefer to dress in certain ways, so we prefer to communicate using certain styles. And, just as we can choose to dress differently, so we can all choose to communicate differently. Most of us can alter our communication style quite easily in certain situations. For example, we'd behave quite differently at a funeral and at a birthday party – just as we'd probably dress differently. Changing our behaviour in this way is what the Economist Intelligence Unit report (picking up the clothing metaphor) calls 'tailoring' our communication style. You may not be able to change your personality; but you can choose to behave differently.

Social: Connecting to others
('pull'; empathizing)

The Social style seeks to understand other people, so that we can improve our relationships with them. We use the Social style to discover what people are thinking and feeling. This style foregrounds listening over speaking, and asking questions over making statements. When we make statements in this style, we use language that expresses emotions openly and connects to other people.

The Social style is the style of the diplomat. When you display this style, people will turn to you as the team player, the consensus-builder, the peacemaker. Indeed, this style is conflict-averse and may not be able to deal with personal criticism easily. And criticism might come from people working in other styles: the Analytical style, for instance, may become irritated with Social's 'touchy-feely' approach. Under pressure, the Social style might become upset and exasperated.

Analytical: Doing the research
('pull'; systemizing)

The Analytical style seeks to understand the environment better. We use this style to understand how things work in the world. This style likes data, numbers and systems for organizing them. It might become irritated with people who can't support their opinions with hard evidence. Like the Social style, Analytical foregrounds listening – or observing – over speaking. Analytical will pick up the trends and underlying causes of events that others might miss. When Analytical speaks, it uses specific, unemotional language – especially the language of measurement or definition.

Analytical is the style of the researcher. People turn to Analytical for clear, dispassionate, logical answers to hard questions. Like Social, Analytical tends to avoid conflict and may therefore find it hard to make a tough decision. Others might call this 'analysis paralysis'. When confronted with such criticism, Analytical may become terse and even rude.

Functional: Making it work ('push'; systemizing)

The Functional style seeks to get things done in the world. We use this style to achieve practical results. Functional prioritizes speaking over listening. It generates and explains processes: timelines, plans, and deliverables.

Functional is the style of the implementer. People turn to this style to make things happen, on time and on budget. The Functional style covers all the details. It may become irritated with the Social style because it's more interested in processes than people. It may ally itself with the Analytical style but become impatient with its hesitation to act. Because it focuses on systems, other styles may find Functional cold, unresponsive or – worst of all – boring. The Functional style can therefore lose people's attention in presentations or meetings.

Expressive: Putting on a show ('push'; empathizing)

The Expressive style seeks to make an impression on other people. We use the Expressive style to present, perform and inspire. This style creates the big picture, using images and stories. Expressive foregrounds speaking over listening; it thinks imaginatively and laterally.

When we use the Expressive style, we're seeking to engage our audience; indeed, we'll tend to see other people principally as an audience rather than a partner in a conversation. An Expressive speaker is acutely aware of how its audience is thinking and feeling – especially about the speaker themselves. The ultimate aim of the Expressive style is to change hearts and minds.

The Expressive style is the style of the visionary. It prefers big ideas to irritating details. It finds its natural home on the podium – or in the pulpit. We call on the Expressive style to tell corporate stories. The Expressive style may find the Analytical style irritating and the Functional style pedestrian. Indeed, the Expressive style may lack the necessary patience to make an informed decision. It may ally itself with the Social style but hijack it for its own ends.

If you've completed this exercise, you'll have a good idea of the way you prefer to communicate. You may come out very strong on just one style; you may find that you combine two as preferred styles. Some people score relatively equally in all four styles; if that's you, then you can congratulate yourself on being a versatile communicator!

Understanding others' styles

Once you've got to know this communication styles model, you can also use it to understand how other people like to communicate.

- People who focus on you and ask you lots of questions are using the Social style.

- People who focus on the task and ask lots of questions about it are using the Analytical style.

- People who make a lot of statements about a task or process are using the Functional style.

- People who use statements to inspire or entertain you are using the Expressive style.

Understanding the style that someone is using will give you clues about how to adapt your own style, so that you can communicate more effectively.

Table 2.1 Understanding others' preferred styles

	Analytical	Functional	Social	Expressive
Fall-back:	Avoids	Resorts to rules	Gives in	Attacks
They value:	Activity and precision	Results and the bottom-line	Attention and friendship	Recognition
They may need to learn how to:	Make decisions	Listen	Initiate action	Check the detail
Manage them best by:	Providing detail	Allowing them to build own structure	Making suggestions and facilitating	Inspiring them to reach their goals
They like to be:	Accurate	Efficient	Agreeable	Stimulating/visionary
Support them with:	Principles and thinking	Conclusion and action	Relationships and feelings	Applause and praise
To help decisions, provide:	Evidence and service	Options and probabilities	Guarantees and assurances	Testimony and incentives

Body language: Non-verbal communication

Conversations, of course, are never simply exchanges of words. We also speak to each other with our bodies – or rather, our bodies often speak for us. Hence the name for this complicated set of behaviours: body language. Some of this language is vocal: the rhythm, tone and volume of our voice, all the grunts, sighs and laughter that surround our words. And some body language is visual: the way we move our eyes or hold someone's gaze, the gestures we use, our posture, the way we move towards or away from another person. All of these elements contribute to our communication style.

What's your preferred body language?

Think about the communication style or styles that you prefer. How does body language contribute to that style? Think about how you use your voice: pace, tonal variation, volume. Think also about how you use your body to express your ideas. Above all, think about what you do with your eyes when you are holding a conversation.

How could you alter your body language to make it more effective?

Body language is largely unconscious. Actors (and con artists) can consciously control their non-verbal behaviour, but it takes a lot of training. Most of us find it hard to manage body language, especially if we're stressed. 'Under pressure,' writes Tracy Cox, 'our bodies leak. Our true feelings come gushing out in gestures.'

Body language can be surprisingly hard to interpret. There are four main reasons for this.

1 **Body language is ambiguous.** No dictionary can accurately define non-verbal signals. Their meaning can vary according to context. Some people close their eyes to concentrate on what you're saying; others do so to try to avoid paying you attention.

2 **Body language is continuous.** We can stop talking but we can't stop our bodies behaving!

3 **Body language is multichannel.** Everything happens at once: eyes, hands, feet, body position. We interpret non-verbal messages holistically, as a complete impression. This makes them strong but unspecific: we may not be able to pin down what the behaviour is suggesting to us.

4 Body language, like any other language, is culturally determined. Research suggests that a few non-verbal messages are universal: everybody seems to smile when they're happy, for example. Most non-verbal behaviours, however, are specific to a culture. A lot of confusion can arise from the misinterpretation of non-verbal messages across a cultural divide.

Our body language, then, can sometimes say things that we don't intend. (Remember that key question in Chapter 1? *What effect am I having?*) We may not know what our bodies are saying; and the other person may be misinterpreting our non-verbal messages.

If you want to work on your non-verbal communication, start with your eyes. If you think more about where you're looking during a conversation, you can find ways to give your words added weight. At its simplest, by looking steadily at the other person and keeping fairly still, you'll probably immediately make the conversation more comfortable.

Key questions: Managing behaviour

- **Look for clusters**
  If you're picking up a group of non-verbal messages that seem to indicate a single feeling, you may be able to trust your interpretation more fully.

- **Consider past experience**
  We can interpret more accurately the behaviour of people we know. We certainly notice changes in their behaviour. We also interpret patterns of behaviour over time more accurately than single instances.

- **Check your perceptions**
  Ask questions. You're interpreting observed behaviour, not reading someone's mind. Check out what you observe and make sure that your interpretation is accurate.

- **Work on your eyes and your gestures**
  Think about where you're looking during the conversation and how you're moving.

Adapting our communication style

We've taken two steps towards making our own communication style more flexible. We have some understanding of our own preferred style, and we're now better able to assess other people's preferred styles. The final step is to find ways of adapting our style to different people and situations.

Effective communicators manage their behaviour. They work hard to align their non-verbal messages with their words. You may feel that altering your behaviour is dishonest or inauthentic: 'play-acting' a part that you don't feel. But – and we return to this hard lesson – the important question is not what we feel, but what *effect* we're having. Managing our behaviour simply means trying to act appropriately: trying to have the right effect on the other person.

Exercise

Here's a thought experiment. Identify the style in the questionnaire on which you scored *lowest*. Now identify situations in which you would benefit from using that style. What would you need to do to develop your skills in that area? What's the first thing you could do?

Adaptability is our willingness and ability to change our behaviour. We've looked at four styles: Social, Analytical, Functional and Expressive. No one style is naturally more adaptable than another. And we're all able to adapt our styles to some extent. We can usually adapt our style more easily with strangers than with people we know well. For example, imagine being promoted from being a member of a team to leading the team: the communication style that worked with our co-workers will probably need to change when we start to manage them, but the team may find this change of style difficult to interpret or accept.

We can test our ability to adapt our behaviour in situations where we don't *want* to adapt, but *choose* to adapt. Here are some ideas to help you get started.

- If you prefer systemizing styles – Analytical or Functional – you could think about ways of displaying more empathic behaviour. Take a moment to explain how you feel about a situation; spend more time on the relationship by asking the other person how they feel. Put yourself into situations where you can encourage, praise or flatter people.

- If you prefer empathizing styles – Social or Expressive – you might look for opportunities to do more systematic thinking. You might need to restrain your social chat or control your enthusiasm. Focus on the task at hand. Make sure you under-stand the elements contributing to a problem, and the steps needed to resolve it.

- If you prefer 'pulling' styles – Analytical or Social – then you could look for opportunities to assert your point of view a little more. Make sure that you make your points simply and clearly; maybe even seek to be a little controversial. Focus on action.

- And if you prefer 'pushing' styles – Functional or Expressive – you could practise listening before speaking, asking for others' views, letting others take control of a conversation and seeking consensus rather than imposing your own views.

Don't try to adapt your style all the time. And think about *how much* you want to adapt your style. The temporary stress of behav-ing in a foreign style might be worth suffering, for the sake of increasing rapport with others. Extreme adaptability, on the other hand, could make you appear inconsistent or dishonest.

Being able to adapt your communication style will bring you multiple benefits at work. Adaptable people interact more productively with everyone they work with. They can manage difficult or tense situations more effectively. They make life easier for everyone.

The uses of conversation

All of the communication styles that we've explored in this chapter reveal themselves in conversation. And all the other modes of communication that we explore in this book are related, in some way, to conversation. In Chapter 4, we look at the skills of enquiry, which build on our powers of listening. And Chapter 5 looks at the complementary skills of persuasion: how we influence each other's thoughts and feelings by speaking. Chapter 6 explores storytelling, and how we can use narrative to explain and persuade more effectively.

Chapters 7 and 8 discuss what we might call 'conversation at a distance'. A presentation, for example, is a conversation in which one person will (probably) speak more than anyone else. And writing is a kind of conversation which lacks most aspects of non-verbal communication. And yet the new technologies – email, texting, instant messaging, social media – are part of a wider trend bringing writing closer to the spoken word, which creates new challenges and the need for new skills.

Finally, in Chapter 9, we look at tough conversations: the ones we might want to avoid, or that erupt suddenly when we least expect them.

But first, let's look a little more at conversation itself: this most powerful and fascinating of communication skills. How can we improve the conversations we hold, at home, at work and in social situations? Chapter 3 provides some suggestions.

Summary points

- We all need to be able to tailor our communication style to different situations and people.

- We can profile our own preferred communication style using two sets of complementary behaviours:
  - pushing and pulling; and
  - empathizing and systemizing.

- Combining these sets of behaviours creates four communication styles:
  - Social;
  - Analytical;
  - Functional; and
  - Expressive.

- Most of us display a preference for one or two of these styles.

- The model also allows us to assess other people's preferred communication styles.

- Our communication style is also displayed by our non-verbal communication or body language: visual gestures and movements; and the tone, volume and speed of our voice.

- Body language can be surprisingly hard to interpret, and we need to check our perceptions of it.

- Effective communicators manage their behaviour.

- Adaptability is our willingness and ability to change our behaviour.

- We can test our ability to adapt our behaviour in situations where we don't *want* to adapt, but *choose* to adapt.

- Don't try to adapt your style all the time.

- Being able to adapt your communication style will bring you multiple benefits at work.

- All of the communication styles that we've explored in this chapter reveal themselves in conversation.

03

Seven ways to improve your conversations

We hold all sorts of conversations at work. Some are relaxed chats (often called 'water-cooler talk'); others are planned. How can we make them more productive?

In this chapter, we look at seven proven strategies.

- Clarify your objective.
- Structure your thinking.
- Manage your time.
- Find common ground.
- Move beyond argument.
- Summarize often.
- Use visuals.

Don't feel that you must apply all seven at once. Take a single strategy and work at it for a few days. (You should have plenty of conversations to practise on!) Once you feel that you have integrated one skill into your conversations, move on to another.

Clarify your objective

Think of a conversation as a journey you are taking with another person. You will both very quickly start to wander off track if you don't know where you're going.

State your objective clearly at the start. Think of this as 'headlining':

I want to talk to you about the development plan.

I know you're worried about the sales figures. I've got some clues that might help.

I've called this meeting to make a decision about project X.

Objectives roughly divide into two categories: 1) exploring a problem; 2) finding a solution. When you're thinking about your headline, ask: 'problem or solution?' We often assume that any conversation about a problem must be aiming to find a solution. As a result, we may find ourselves working towards a solution without accurately defining or understanding the problem. (More on this in the next section, 'Structure your thinking'.)

In a meeting, the best place to announce the objectives of the conversation is on the agenda. That word means 'things to be done'. Use your agenda to list what you want to do in the meeting, not just what you want to talk about. For example, rather than a bald heading such as 'IT infrastructure', write something like 'Review supplier options for IT support and choose preferred bidder'. You have stated the conversation's objective; now everyone in the meeting knows where the conversation should be going.

Of course, you might decide to change your objective in the middle of the conversation – just as you might decide to change direction in the middle of a journey. That's fine, as long as everyone in the conversation knows what's going on. Indeed, if you make your objective too specific at the start of the conversation, you might limit your options for success at the end. In a negotiation, for example, think about different possible destinations: what is your preferred outcome, what would you be willing to settle for, and what's non-negotiable?

Structure your thinking

You can improve your conversations enormously by giving them structure. The simplest way to structure a conversation is to break it into two halves.

We can imagine thinking as a process in two stages. We do *first-stage thinking* when we're working out what we're thinking about; we do *second-stage thinking* when we're working out what to do about it. First-stage thinking explores reality and translates what we've found into language; second-stage thinking then manipulates the language to decide what to do. We could say that first-stage thinking is perception, and second-stage thinking is judgement.

We often ignore first-stage thinking. We may assume that we know what we're looking at. But, of course, the quality of our second-stage thinking depends directly on the quality of our first-stage thinking. If our perception of a situation is limited, then our judgement about it will be limited. If we misunderstand a problem, then we may come up with a poor solution.

I sometimes think that we can focus too hard, and too quickly, on solutions. Under pressure of time and the drive for results, we leap to second-stage thinking without spending nearly enough time in the first stage. We don't explore the problems we're trying to solve. Indeed, we may not want to look too long at a problem; better, we might think, to deal with it and push it out of the way. (Or, maybe, simply ignore it and hope that it will disappear.)

However troubling the problem may be, try to explore it as fully as possible. Give first-stage thinking as much time and attention as you can.

Then give it a little more. And make sure that all participants in the conversation are at the same stage of thinking at the same time.

> ## Top tip
>
> In meetings, invite and encourage different views of the problem
> from different participants – especially from group members who
> may not be speaking very much. You may be straying into
> delicate or controversial areas, but the wider the range of views
> you have, the more richly you'll understand the problem.

The trick is to find the link between the two stages of thinking. Skilled conversationalists work on linking:

- the past and the present;
- the problem and the solution;
- requests and answers;
- negative ideas and positive ideas;
- opinions about what is true with speculation about the consequences.

Four types of conversation

We can break down the two stages of thinking into four conversations. These are conversations for:

- relationship;
- possibility;
- opportunity;
- action.

These four conversations may form part of a single, larger conversation; they may also take place separately, at different stages of a process or project (see Figure 3.1).

Figure 3.1   Four conversations

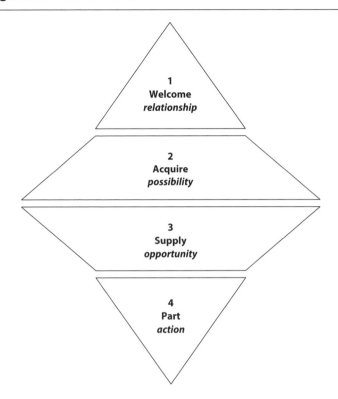

A conversation for relationship

This conversation lays the foundation for the other three. We hold this conversation to create or develop the relationship we need, in order to achieve our objective.

Key questions in this conversation will include:

- *Who are we?*
- *What is the problem?*
- *How do you define the problem?*
- *How do we relate to the matter in hand?*
- *What links us?*
- *How do we see things?*

- *What do you see that I cannot see?*
- *What do I see that you do not see?*
- *In what ways do we see things similarly, or differently?*

Conversations for relationship may be tentative, awkward or embarrassing. We often rush them. Think of those tricky conversations we hold with strangers at parties. A good conversation for relationship moves beyond the 'What do you do? Where do you live?' questions. We are defining our relationship to each other, and how we see the matter in hand.

A conversation for possibility

A conversation for possibility continues the exploration: it develops first-stage thinking. It asks what we *might* be looking at.

Exercise

Key questions in a conversation for possibility include:

- *What is the real problem?*
- *What are we really trying to do?*
- *Is this a problem?*
- *How could we look at this from a different angle?*
- *Can we interpret this differently?*
- *How could we do this?*
- *What does it look like from another person's point of view?*
- *What makes this different from last time?*
- *Have we ever done anything like this before?*
- *Can we make this simpler?*
- *Can we look at this in bits?*
- *What is this like?*
- *What does this feel or look like?*

A conversation for possibility is *not* about whether to do something, or what to do. It seeks to find new ways of looking at the problem.

And, in fact, we could look at any problem in lots of different ways. If you are stuck with a problem, try one of these strategies.

- Look at it from a new angle.
- Ask for different interpretations of what is happening.
- Try to distinguish what you are looking at from what you think about it.
- Ask how other people might see it.
- Break the problem into parts.
- Isolate one part of the problem and look at it in detail.
- Connect the problem into a wider network of ideas.
- Ask what the problem is like. What does it look like, or feel like?

Conversations for possibility can be very creative: brainstorming is a good example. But exploring different points of view can also create conflict: what Edward de Bono calls 'adversarial thinking'. (More about adversarial thinking shortly, and in Chapter 9.)

This isn't decision time. If you're chairing a meeting, for example, encourage people to give you ideas, and take care not to judge or criticize either the ideas or the person. Manage the emotional content of this conversation with particular care. When someone makes an emotional comment, ask – gently – for the evidence.

A conversation for opportunity

A conversation for opportunity takes us into second-stage thinking.

Key questions in this conversation include:

- *Where can we act?*
- *What could we do?*
- *Which possibilities do we build on?*
- *Which possibilities are feasible?*

- *What target do we set ourselves?*
- *Where are the potential obstacles?*
- *How will we know that we have succeeded?*

This conversation focuses on future action: in choosing from among a number of possibilities, you're finding a sense of common purpose. So this conversation is about planning. Many of our good ideas never become reality because we don't map out paths of opportunity. A conversation for opportunity constructs such a path. Assess what you would need to make action possible: resources, support and skills.

Top tip

The bridge from possibility to opportunity is measurement. Begin to set targets and measures of success. If you're talking about a project, where are the milestones – and the obstacles? And how will you measure success?

Backward planning can often be more effective than forward planning. Recall your original objective. Has it changed? Place yourselves in a future where you've achieved your objective. What does such a future look like? What's happening? What do you need to do to create that future? Backward planning may allow you to simplify the plan and find new opportunities for action.

A conversation for action

In this conversation, you agree what to do, who will do it and when it will happen. Translating opportunity into action needs more than agreement; you need to generate a promise, a *commitment* to act.

A conversation for action is essential at the end of an interview or meeting. After all, if nothing happens as a result of these conversations, why hold them? A conversation for action balances asking and promising. If necessary, take this conversation step by step.

How to hold a conversation for action

1   Ask the other person to do something by a certain time. Make it clear that this is a request, not an order. Orders may get immediate results, but they rarely generate commitment.

2   The other person now has four possible answers to this request:

   –   They can accept.

   –   They can decline.

   –   They may commit to accepting or declining at a later date. (*'I'll let you know by…'*)

   –   They can make a counter-offer. (*'I can't do that, but I can do…'*)

3   Negotiate until the other person is able to make a firm promise. *'I will do x for you by time y.'*

The person making the promise should use this precise wording. Don't settle for a simple 'Yes, I'll do that.' If they *specify* what they will do, and by when – and if they themselves write that action down – then they are more likely to do it. Use this technique to gain commitment to actions at the end of a meeting. If people promise to do something, publicly, and write it down, they are more likely to do what they promise.

These four conversations will only be truly effective if you hold them *in order*. The success of each conversation depends on the success of the conversation before it. If you fail to resolve a conversation, it will continue underneath the next *in code*. Unresolved aspects of a conversation for relationship, for instance, can become conflicts of possibility, hidden agendas or 'personality clashes'. Possibilities left unexplored become lost opportunities. And promises to act that have no real commitment behind them may mean that things don't get done.

Manage your time

Conversations take time, and time is our one entirely non-renewable resource.

Managing time for the conversation

Work out how much time you have. Don't just assume that there's no time. Be realistic. If necessary, make an appointment to hold the interview later, or schedule the meeting for another time.

Top tip

Always be ready to ask the other person if this is a good time to hold this conversation – and how much time they have.

Managing time in the conversation

Most conversations speed up and slow down at different times. Generally, an effective conversation will probably start quite slowly and get faster as it goes on. But there are no hard and fast rules about this.

Conversations can go too fast for all sorts of reasons. Paradoxically, agreement and conflict can both cause conversations to speed up. You may have settled on a solution too quickly or have succumbed to 'groupthink' (in which everyone agrees because it feels comforting to agree). Alternatively, a disagreement may have flared into an emotional argument.

Conversely, conversations can become painfully slow when we find ourselves stuck with a problem (or with only one view of a problem). If you hear people analysing the past instead of looking to the future, or people wandering off the subject, it's likely that you need to inject the conversation with new energy.

Exercise

Spend a morning monitoring the pace of your conversations. Which ones went too fast? Which were too slow? During the afternoon, continue monitoring but take action to adjust the pace of the conversation. If the conversation is going too slowly, close down sections of the conversation by summarizing; push for action or move from remarks to implications: 'what does this mean in terms of...?' If the conversation is going too fast, slow it down by reflecting or paraphrasing before responding, by asking open questions (questions beginning with one of the 'w' words – 'why?' is a good candidate) or by simply pausing.

Find common ground

The most satisfying conversations create the sense that we've found common ground. We may have each started in our own territory, with our own points of view; by the end of the conversation, we've found the place where we can stand together, facing the future. To find that place, we may need to move: to change our position, to shift our point of view. Conversation – moving around together – is the means by which we achieve that.

We ask for, and give, permission for these moves to happen. If you're asking permission to move into new territory, you might:

- make a remark tentatively;
- express yourself hesitantly ('Perhaps we might...' 'I suppose I think...' 'It's possible that...');
- pause before speaking;
- look away or look down a lot;
- explicitly ask permission ('Do you mind if I mention...' 'May I speak freely about...');

- make a tentative remark about the other person's words or behaviour.

Don't proceed until the other person has given their permission. They might do so explicitly ('Please say what you like'; 'I would really welcome your honest opinion'; 'I don't mind you talking about that'). Or they might give permission without using words: nodding, smiling, leaning forward.

Conversely, refusing permission can be explicit – 'I'd rather we didn't talk about this' – or in code. The person may evade your question, answer vaguely or reply with another question. Their non-verbal behaviour may hint at their real feelings: folding their arms, sitting back in the chair, becoming restless, evading eye contact.

Move beyond argument

Ask anyone what they think of something, and the chances are they'll tell you what's wrong with it. Too often, we assume that the only way to explore someone else's idea is to argue against it. Adversarial thinking seems to be deeply engrained in us, perhaps because so many of us learn the skills of debating at school.

A debate is like a verbal boxing match. (The word derives from Latin, 'to beat down'). By the rules of debate, your opinions are somehow proved to be correct if you can successfully discredit any opposing opinions. You don't even have to prove that an idea is wrong; merely by ridiculing or discrediting the person voicing it, you may be able to persuade others that you are right. (This is sometimes called an *ad hominem* argument.)

But argument – however formally conducted – *stops* us exploring and discovering new ideas. And argument can threaten the quality of the conversation itself by raising its emotional temperature: people can become too busy defending themselves, too frightened, too battle fatigued, to do any better.

> **Top tip**
>
> Next time you're asked to comment on an idea, deliberately ask yourself: 'What's good about this idea?'

The ladder of inference

The 'ladder of inference' (Figure 3.2) takes our conversations beyond argument. The model was developed by Chris Argyris, and develops the principle of pattern-matching, which we explored in Chapter 1, into a set of steps on a ladder. We pattern-match on each step. At the bottom of the ladder is observation; at the top, action.

- From our observation, we step onto the first rung of the ladder by selecting *data*. (We choose what to look at.)

- On the second rung, we infer meaning from our experience of similar data.

- On the third rung, we generalize those meanings into *assumptions*.

- On the fourth rung, we construct mental models (or *beliefs*) out of those assumptions.

- We act on the basis of our mental models.

We travel up and down this ladder whenever we hold a conversation. We're often much better at climbing up than stepping down; in fact, we can leap up all the rungs in a few seconds. These 'leaps of abstraction' allow us to act more quickly, but they can also limit the scope of the conversation by creating a belief or mental model that limits our thinking. These beliefs can also send us back *down* the ladder and filter our observations – we select only the data that fits our belief. Argyris calls this a 'reflexive loop'; we might also call it a mindset.

Figure 3.2   The ladder of inference

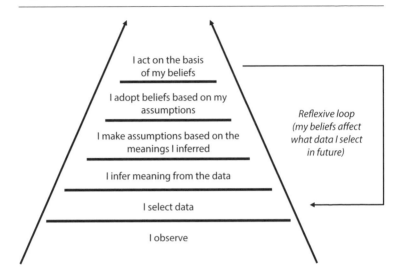

The ladder of inference gives us more choices about where to go in a conversation. It *slows down* our thinking. It allows us to:

- become more aware of our own thinking;
- make that thinking available to others;
- ask others about their thinking.

Above all, we can defuse an adversarial conversation by 'climbing down' from private beliefs, assumptions and opinions and then 'climbing up' to shared meanings and beliefs.

The key to using the ladder of inference is to ask questions.

- *What is the data that underlies what you have said?*
- *Do we agree on the data?*
- *Do we agree on what they mean?*
- *Can you take me through your reasoning?*
- *When you say [what you have said], do you mean [my rewording of it]?*

For example, if one of us suggests a course of action, the other can carefully climb down the ladder by asking:

- *'Why do you think this might work?' 'What makes this a good plan?'*

- *'What assumptions do you think you might be making?' 'Have you considered...?'*

- *'How would this affect...?' 'Does this mean that...?'*

- *'Can you give me an example?' 'What led you to look at this in particular?'*

Even more powerfully, the ladder of inference can help us to offer our own thinking for the other person to examine. If we're suggesting a plan of action, we can ask them:

- *'Can you see any flaws in my thinking?'*

- *'Would you look at this stuff differently?' 'How would you put this together?'*

- *'Would this look different in different circumstances?' 'Are my assumptions valid?'*

- *'Have I missed anything?'*

The beauty of the ladder of inference is that you don't need any special training to use it. You can use it immediately, as a practical way to intervene in conversations that may be collapsing into argument.

Exercise

Draw a picture of the ladder of inference on a piece of paper and add some of the questions listed above, near different rungs of the ladder. Put the paper in your wallet or bag – somewhere you can find it easily. Next time you find yourself disagreeing with someone in a conversation, take out the paper and use it to try, deliberately, to climb up or down the ladder. Ask questions; test assumptions; show the links in your own thinking; and ask the other person to show the links in theirs. See where the conversation goes. Then reflect on how useful the ladder of inference was as a conversation tool.

Summarize often

Summaries help us to do everything else we have been discussing in this chapter. They allow us to state our objective and check that we both share the same one. They allow us to structure the conversation and check where we are in our journey through first- and second-stage thinking. They help us to manage time and seek common ground; and they can help us to defuse argument.

Summarizing is not merely repeating what the other person has just said. To summarize means to reinterpret their ideas in your own language. It involves:

- *recognizing* the specific point they have made;
- *appreciating* the position from which they say it;
- *understanding* the beliefs that inform that position.

Recognizing what someone says does not imply that you agree with it. It *does* imply that you're thinking about what they've said. Appreciating their feelings does not mean you feel the same way, but it *does* show that you recognize those feelings. And understanding what they believe may not mean that you share their belief; but it *does* mean that you respect it. All of which means that summaries can contribute to shared problem solving.

Top tip

At the end of a conversation, co-create a summary with the other person.

Use visuals

Many of our conversations have a visual element. Often that element is expressed in our bodies: the way our hand gestures and facial expressions enrich the meaning of our words. And we can use tools to make our thinking visible: scribbling on the back of an envelope, building a model or running a demonstration.

Meetings, in particular, benefit hugely from using visual tools. A meeting is a group of people thinking together; when we can all see what we're thinking about, we think more efficiently, effectively – and collaboratively. The visual aid focuses our thinking – literally – and we're less inclined to wander off the topic. And, the more interactive the visual tool, the more it can help us generate new ideas. A huge range of tools are available: flipcharts and sketchpads, notepads and sticky notes, whiteboards and smartboards, slide decks and interactive screens.

We may be using these tools far more as meetings go online. Visual aids can certainly make meetings more disciplined, more inclusive and more enjoyable. And they don't have to be high tech.

Mind maps are a powerful way to visualize our thinking. In particular, they help us to do first-stage thinking – linking elements and encouraging us to find new ways of looking at something. Mind maps can not only record our thinking, but also improve it.

Exercise

Use this exercise the next time you need to organize your thoughts about a project, a report or a presentation:

1 Put a visual image of your subject at the centre of a plain piece of paper.

2 Write down anything that comes to mind that connects to the central idea. Don't edit or block any ideas; every idea has the potential to be useful.

3 Write single words, in BLOCK CAPITALS, along lines radiating from the centre.

  Main ideas will tend to gravitate to the centre of the map; details will radiate towards the edge.

Every line must connect to at least one other line.

Use visual display: colour, pattern, highlights.

Identify the groups of ideas that you have created. If you wish, give each a heading and put the groups into a number order.

Try out mind maps – in relatively simple conversations to begin with. Record a phone conversation using a mind map and see how well you get on with the technique. Extend your practice to face-to-face conversations and invite the other person to look at and contribute to the map. Many managers use them to record meetings, and as the notes for minute writing. Software packages make it possible to create mind maps on screen – a particular benefit for online meetings.

Using metaphors

Many of the most powerful visuals are created with the words we use. In particular, we can use metaphors. Metaphors are images of ideas in concrete form. The word means 'transferring' or 'carrying over': a metaphor carries your meaning from one thing to another. It enables your listener to see something in a new way, by picturing it as something else.

We use many metaphors without even noticing them. If you want to extend your use of metaphors, start by listening out for them in your everyday conversations.

Exercise

Here is a useful exercise to open up your thinking about a problem. It is especially helpful if you are completely stuck and cannot find any solution.

1 Start by writing down the problem. You could define the problem either as a statement of what is wrong, or as a 'how to'.

2 For example, the problem might be either 'the team isn't working well together' or 'how to help the team work better together'.

3 Now ask yourself these questions:

   – What is the problem like?

   – If this were a different situation – a game of cricket, a medieval castle, a mission to Mars, a kindergarten – how would we deal with it?

   – How would a different kind of person manage the issue: a gardener, a politician, an engineer, a hairdresser, an actor?

   – What does this situation feel like?

   – If this problem were an animal, what species of animal would it be?

   – Describe the problem as if it were part of the human body.

4 Now try to find connections from the metaphors you have discovered back to the original problem. What does a metaphor suggest about future actions?

You probably need to slow down the conversation to find these metaphors. You'll know when you've found a productive metaphor. ('Found' in that sentence is a metaphor.) The conversation will suddenly catch fire (that's another metaphor!). You'll feel a sudden injection of energy (and there's a third metaphor) as you realize that you are looking at the issue in a completely new way.

Summary points

- There are seven proven strategies to help you to improve your conversations:
  - clarify your objective;
  - structure your thinking;
  - manage your time;
  - find common ground;
  - move beyond argument;
  - summarize often;
  - use visuals.
- To clarify your objective:
  - state your objective clearly at the start;
  - ask: problem or solution?
- To structure your thinking:
  - use first-stage thinking and second-stage thinking;
  - hold conversations for: relationship, possibility, opportunity, action.
- To manage your time:
  - manage time for the conversation;
  - manage time in the conversation.
- To find common ground:
  - ask for permission to move onto the other person's territory;
  - give permission for the other person to move onto your territory.

- To move beyond argument:
  - use the ladder of inference to check the other person's thinking;
  - use the ladder of inference to invite the other person to check your thinking.
- Summarize:
  - at the start of the conversation;
  - regularly throughout the conversation;
  - at the end of the conversation.
- Use visuals:
  - record your ideas;
  - use mind maps;
  - use metaphors.

04
The skills of enquiry

The skills of enquiry are the skills of listening. On the 'push'/'pull' spectrum that we explored in Chapter 2, listening is a core 'pulling' behaviour. And the quality of any conversation depends on the quality of the listening.

Stephen Covey famously said: 'Seek first to understand, then to be understood.' Only by enquiring into someone's ideas can you respond honestly and fully to them. Only by discovering how they think can you begin to persuade them to your way of thinking. Only by listening can you begin to manage and lead them.

But skilled enquiry also helps the person you're listening to. Listening – real, deep, attentive listening – can help them to think better.

I've summarized the skills of enquiry under seven headings:

- paying attention;
- treating the speaker as an equal;
- cultivating ease;
- encouraging;
- asking quality questions;
- rationing information;
- giving positive feedback.

Acquiring these skills will help you to give the other person the respect and space they deserve in order to develop their own ideas – to make their thinking visible.

Paying attention

Paying attention is one of the most respectful things we can do. Paying attention means concentrating on what someone is saying. That sounds simple: how can we listen without paying attention?

Of course, we often do just that. Nancy Kline puts it well, in her book, *Time to Think*:

> *We think we listen, but we don't. We finish each other's sentences, we interrupt each other, we moan together, we fill in the pauses with our own stories, we look at our watches, we sigh, frown, tap our finger, read the newspaper, or walk away. We give advice, give advice, give advice.*

Real listening means pausing our own thinking and allowing the speaker's thinking to enter our mind.

Paying attention helps a speaker to find their ideas and express them. If we're paying proper attention, the speaker will become more articulate. And if we're not paying attention, they'll stumble and hesitate. Poor attention makes them more stupid; close attention makes them more intelligent.

Don't rush. Adjust your own tempo to that of the other person. Wait longer than you want to. And when they can't think of anything else to say, ask: 'What else do you think about this? What else can you think of? What else comes to mind?' That invitation to talk more can bring even the weariest brain back to life.

Interrupting

Interrupting is the most obvious symptom of poor attention. Sometimes, we can't resist it. Some demon inside us seems to compel us to fill the speaker's pauses with words. It's as if the very idea of silence terrifies us.

Mostly, we interrupt because we're making assumptions. Next time you interrupt someone in a conversation, ask yourself which of these assumptions you are applying.

- My idea is better than theirs.
- The answer is more important than the problem.
- I have to utter my idea fast and if I don't interrupt, I'll lose my chance (or forget it).
- I know what they are going to say.
- They don't need to finish the sentence because my rewrite is an improvement.
- They can't improve this idea any further, so I might as well improve it for them.
- I'm more important than they are.
- It is more important for me to be seen to have a good idea than for me to let them finish.
- Interrupting will save time.

If you're assuming you know what the speaker is about to say, you're probably wrong. If you allow them to continue, they will often come up with something more interesting, more vivid and more personal.

Exercise

Next time you hold a conversation with a colleague, deliberately note down the number of times you interrupt them – and the number of times they interrupt you. When the conversation has finished, count up the two totals. What do the numbers suggest? How many of those interruptions were useful or necessary? (Not every interruption is unhelpful.)

Allowing quiet

Once you stop interrupting, the conversation will become quieter. Pauses will appear. The other person will stop talking and you will not fill the silence.

Think of these pauses as junctions in your conversation's journey. You have a number of choices about where you might go next. Either of you might choose. If you want to switch from listening to persuading, you might make the choice. But, if you're enquiring, then you give the speaker the privilege of making the choice.

Top tip

There are two kinds of pause. One is a filled pause; the other is empty. Learn to distinguish between the two.

Some pauses are filled with thought. Sometimes, the speaker will stop, perhaps suddenly. They'll look elsewhere, probably into a longer distance. They are busy on an excursion – and you're not invited. But they will want you to be there at the junction when they come back. They have trusted you to wait. So wait.

The other kind of pause is an empty one. Nothing much is happening. The speaker does not stop suddenly; instead, they seem to fade away. You're standing at the junction in the conversation together, and neither of you is moving. The energy seems to drop out of the conversation. The speaker's eyes don't focus anywhere. If they're comfortable in your company, they may focus on you as a cue for you to choose what move to make.

Wait out the pause. If the pause is empty, the speaker will probably say so in a few moments. 'I can't think of anything else.' 'That's it, really.' 'So. There we are. I'm stuck now.' Try asking: 'Can you think of anything else?' If the other person is ready for you to take the lead, then do so: ask a question, make a suggestion.

Showing that you are paying attention

The best way to look as if you are paying attention is – well, to pay attention. But sometimes we need to consciously work at paying attention. Begin with your eyes: practise looking steadily at the speaker when you're listening to them, and start to notice when you glance away. Generally, we don't look nearly enough at the people we listen to.

Working on our eye movements benefits both listener and speaker. If you look more attentively, you'll actually pay more attention to what the speaker is saying. (The speaker will probably look away from you more frequently; it's what we do when we're thinking about what to say.) Relax your facial muscles: no frowns or rigid smiles. Use minimal encouragers (more about those in the section on 'encouraging' below.) But come back, always, to the way you use your eyes.

Be aware that such attentive looking may actually inhibit the speaker. In some cultures, looking equates to staring and signals disrespect. You need to be sensitive to these possible individual or cultural distinctions and adapt your eye movements accordingly.

Treating the speaker as an equal

You'll enquire well only if you raise the other person's status. 'Pushing' behaviour, which raises our status, will always lower the other person's status (look back at Chapter 2). That will interrupt their thinking, and may mean that you never discover valuable information and ideas.

For managers and leaders, status in conversations is often complicated by power. Power can come in many different forms: the power to reward or punish, for example; the power deriving from regulation or expertise; the power conferred by a senior role. When power combines with status-raising 'push' behaviours, we can easily find ourselves becoming patronizing.

Patronizing the speaker is the greatest enemy of equality in conversations. It grows out of the way parents and carers treat children (the word comes from the Latin word 'pater', meaning 'father'). Of course, we often have to treat children like children. We need to:

- direct them;
- control them;
- think for them.

If you're a manager, you might see that list as a more or less comprehensive list of your responsibilities towards the people you manage. And you might think that the way to discharge those responsibilities is to talk. But wise managers – and leaders – know that there's far more to be gained from listening than from talking.

As soon as you think you know better than the other person, or provide the answers for them, you're patronizing them. You cannot patronize someone and pay them close attention at the same time.

Cultivating ease

Good thinking happens in a relaxed environment. Cultivating ease will allow you to enquire more deeply, and discover more ideas. When you are at ease, the solution to a problem will sometimes appear as if by magic.

Many people are uncomfortable with the idea of ease at work. They're so used to urgency that they cannot imagine working in any other way. Many organizations equate ease with sloth. If you're not working flat out, chasing deadlines and juggling 50 assignments at the same time, you're not worth your salary. It's sometimes assumed that the best thinking happens in such a climate.

Not so. Urgency keeps people from thinking well; they're too busy *doing*. After all, doing is what gets results, isn't it? Well, not when people have to think to get those results. Sometimes, the best results only appear by *not* doing: by paying attention to someone else's ideas with a mind that's alert and at ease.

Cultivating ease is a behavioural skill. You don't have to *feel* at ease to promote ease in another person. (How would you speak to a person who is threatening you with a gun, for example?) Breathe out, slow down your speaking rhythm, lower the volume and the pitch of your voice. Banish distractions: unplug the phone, close the door, find somewhere quiet and comfortable. (You may need to leave the office.) Make time. If the time isn't right, postpone the conversation.

Encouraging

In order to liberate the other person's ideas, you may need to do more than pay attention, treat them as an equal and cultivate ease. You may need to actively encourage them to give you their ideas.

We're back with that key question we discovered in Chapter 1: *What effect am I having?* The speaker's thinking is largely the result of the effect you are having on them. So if you:

- suggest that they change the subject;

- try to convince them of your point of view before listening to their point of view;

- reply tit-for-tat to their remarks; or

- encourage them to compete with you,

you're not encouraging them to develop their thinking. You're not enquiring properly.

One of the worst enemies of encouragement is competitiveness. We can easily find ourselves using the speaker's ideas to promote our own. It's all part of that habit of adversarial thinking.

Competition forces people to think only those thoughts that will help them win. If the speaker feels that you're competing with them, they'll not only say less, but think less. Conversely, if you feel that the speaker is trying to compete with you, don't allow yourself to enter the competition. The ladder of inference (see Chapter 3) is one very powerful tool that will help you to defuse competitiveness in your conversations.

Instead of competing, welcome the difference in your points of view. Then try to find common ground. (Look back at Chapter 3.)

Minimal encouragers

Minimal encouragers are brief, supportive actions that show the speaker that you want them to continue. They can be:

- sub-vocalizations: 'uh-huh', 'mm';
- words and phrases: 'right', 'really?', 'I see';
- repeated key words.

Behaviours can include:

- leaning forward;
- focusing eye contact;
- head nodding.

Minimal encouragers support the speaker without interrupting them. They demonstrate your interest, both generally and in particular points that the speaker is making. But beware: they could subtly influence the speaker to say what they think you want to hear, rather than what they want to say. And, poorly used, they can signal impatience or become an empty gesture.

Asking quality questions

Questions are at the heart of enquiry. That's obvious: enquiring *is* asking a question.

But, of course, questions can do much more than enquire. We can use them to spark an argument or to make ourselves look clever. Questions can be statements in disguise; we can use them to criticize, ridicule or even insult.

It's not always considered good form to ask questions. We may stop ourselves asking a question because we fear challenging authority, or looking stupid. In some organizations, asking questions is simply 'not done'. 'Questioning,' said Samuel Johnson on one occasion, 'is not the mode of conversation among gentlemen.' (I assume that he was being ironic.)

The best questions open up the speaker's thinking. A question that helps them to think further, develop an idea or clarify a thought, is a high-quality question. So use questions to:

- find out facts;
- check your understanding;
- help the other person to improve their understanding;
- invite the other person to examine your own thinking;
- request action.

A whole repertoire of questions is available to help you to enquire more fully. Specifically, we can use six types of questions.

- *Closed questions* can only be answered 'yes' or 'no'.
- *Open questions* cannot be answered 'yes' or 'no'.
- *Leading questions* put the answer into the other person's mouth.
- *Controlling questions* help you to take the lead in the conversation.
- *Probing questions* build on an earlier question, or dig deeper.
- *Reflecting questions* restate the last remark but with no new request.

The ladder of inference can provide all sorts of questions. You can also use it to invite the speaker to ask you questions.

One particular kind of question is especially powerful. It can liberate the speaker's thinking by removing the assumptions that limit it. This magic question starts with two words: 'What if'.

Guess an assumption that the speaker might be making and then ask either, 'What if this assumption weren't true?' or 'What if the opposite assumption were true?'

Examples of the first kind of question might include:

- *What if you became chief executive tomorrow?*
- *What if I weren't your manager?*
- *What if you weren't limited in your use of equipment?*

Examples of the second kind might include:

- *What if you weren't limited by a budget?*
- *What if customers were actually flocking to us?*
- *What if you knew that you were vital to the company's success?*

Exercise

Next time you prepare for a fact-finding conversation – an appraisal interview, perhaps, or a project update – make a list of the questions you could ask. Try to include at least one of every type: closed, open, leading, controlling, probing, reflecting, 'what if'. Think about a possible order for these questions, and how some questions might be alternatives or potential questions, depending on the direction the conversation takes.

Rationing information

Information is power. Withholding information can be a power move, putting you at an advantage over the other person. But offering *too much* information can also interfere with enquiry: it can stop the other person thinking effectively. So it helps, in enquiry mode, to *ration* the information you give.

- *Don't interrupt.* Let the speaker finish before giving any new information. Don't force information into the middle of their sentence.

- *Time your intervention.* Ask yourself when the most appropriate time might be to offer the information.

- *Filter the information.* Only offer information that you think will improve the speaker's thinking. Resist the temptation to amplify some piece of information that's not central to their thinking.

- *Don't give information to show off.* You may be tempted to give information to demonstrate how expert or up to date you are. Resist that temptation.

Top tip

Ask the other person what information they need to know before you start to offer what *you* think they need to know.

You can also ration the amount of information you ask the speaker to give you. Ask for information at the right time and for the right reason; better to let the speaker work out their own ideas and then ask for a summary, than to keep interrupting them with questions.

Giving positive feedback

At its simplest, we use feedback to check that we've understood. But feedback can do more: it can help us to switch from listening to speaking – from enquiry to persuasion, perhaps. It can prepare us to move from first-stage to second-stage thinking, from problem to solution. And feedback can reinforce the speaker's sense of self-worth, which can lead to improved performance.

For many managers, of course, feedback is often not the *result* of a listening conversation, but the *reason* for holding the conversation in the first place. Many managers find performance feedback stressful, especially if they fear a hostile response from the employee. In the survey commissioned by the Interact consultancy in 2016, over a third of managers (37 per cent) claimed to feel uncomfortable giving performance feedback to which the employee might respond negatively.

This anxiety impels the manager to get through the meeting as quickly as possible. That's understandable: we're programmed to avoid pain. But the result is a conversation in which the manager does nearly all the talking and the employee remains silent. It's all 'push': no enquiry, no listening, no real attention.

Now consider the effect of this conversation on the employee. In a survey of almost 4,000 people, Jack Zenger and Joseph Folkman found that people's attitude to feedback alters significantly according to how well they feel listened to. The less people felt their managers listened to them, the more likely they were to believe that the feedback was dishonest. In particular, employees who felt that their managers didn't listen to them were significantly less happy to receive negative feedback.

The conclusion's clear. Performance feedback works best when the manager begins by listening to the employee.

Top tip

Consider the classic opening line of a feedback meeting: 'Come in and close the door, I want to talk to you.' Imagine it rewritten as: 'Please come in and close the door; I want to listen to you.'

Whether you're managing or not, the best kind of feedback is *genuine*, *succinct* and *specific*. And, of course, it can have those qualities only if you've listened well.

Choose carefully when to give your feedback. If in doubt, ask whether it is appropriate to start your feedback or whether the speaker wants to continue. Ask:

- for permission to feed back;
- how the speaker sees the situation in summary;
- what the speaker sees as the key issue or problem.

Only then should you launch into your own feedback.

Balancing appreciation and criticism

There are two kinds of feedback: positive and negative.

We often assume that negative feedback is more realistic than positive feedback. 'Get real', we might say to justify criticism. We might assume that positive feedback – saying what we like about an idea – is naive and simplistic. Years of training and experience in critical thinking may have taught us not to comment on what we approve or like.

Actually, of course, the positive aspects of reality can be just as realistic as the negative ones. Adding positive feedback to the negative doesn't distort our view of reality; it adds to it.

Top tip

You can discover a source of positive feedback simply by asking yourself, 'What's good about this idea?' You could even ask the speaker the same question. The answer will nearly always reveal something that you had not noticed before. And that can form the basis for positive feedback.

We can transform negative into positive feedback by using the phrase 'how to'. For example, if the other person is suggesting doing something and you want to say, 'We simply don't have the resources to do this', you could rephrase the remark by asking 'How could we do this with the limited resources we have?' If you want to say 'You haven't thought this through', you could ask 'How can we develop this idea more thoroughly?'

Those two simple words – 'how to' – can have a magical effect on the quality of your feedback.

Exercise

Spend one day noting down all your responses to ideas from other people. How many times were your comments negative – in other words, expressing what you didn't like about something or what you thought was wrong with the idea? How many comments were positive – expressing what you liked about the idea or what you thought was good about it? How could you transform the negative comments into positive ones? Could you, for example, turn a criticism into a 'how could we' question?

Summary points

- There are seven key skills of enquiry:
  - paying attention;
  - treating the speaker as an equal;
  - cultivating ease;
  - encouraging;
  - asking quality questions;
  - rationing information;
  - giving positive feedback.
- To pay attention:
  - listen;
  - don't interrupt;
  - allow quiet;
  - show that you are paying attention.

- To treat the speaker as an equal:
  - give equal turns to speak and listen;
  - don't tell them what to say;
  - don't assume that you know what they mean better than they do.
- To cultivate ease:
  - find time;
  - make space;
  - banish distractions.
- To encourage:
  - don't compete in the conversation;
  - explore differences of opinion;
  - use minimal encouragers.
- Ask quality questions to help you:
  - find out facts;
  - check your understanding;
  - help the other person to improve their understanding;
  - invite the other person to examine your own thinking;
  - request action.
- To ration information:
  - don't interrupt;
  - time your intervention;
  - filter the information;
  - don't give information to show off.
- To give positive feedback:
  - balance appreciation and criticism;
  - assume constructive intent;
  - feed back on specifics.

05
The skills of persuasion

The ability to persuade has never been in more demand. Anyone who can win hearts and minds will not be out of work for long.

This magical talent has been the subject of study for thousands of years. The classical Greeks called it rhetoric: the earliest manual that survives is by Aristotle. In the Middle Ages and Renaissance, rhetoric was a core part of the curriculum in European schools and universities; Shakespeare's genius, for example, is underpinned by a solid rhetorical training.

Rhetoric shows us that persuasion works both consciously and unconsciously. We might call the unconscious element 'influence'. (Vance Packard's famous 1957 book, *The Hidden Persuaders*, explored subliminal influence in advertising and the media.) The most successful persuasion will always include a great deal of influencing.

These days, few of us study rhetoric; but the great tradition still has plenty to teach us about influencing and persuading. To return yet again to that first question – *What effect am I having?* – rhetoric teaches us how to employ a wide range of different effects in order to convince our listeners.

Character, logic and passion

Aristotle suggested that persuasion combined three skills. A speaker could appeal to his audience (in classical rhetoric, the speaker was almost always male) by enhancing his reputation or authority with them; by using logic; and by stirring their emotions. Aristotle famously named these three skills *ethos*, *logos* and *pathos*. He was writing about orators: politicians, lawyers and generals addressing huge crowds of Athenian citizens. But his model has just as much to teach a manager speaking at a meeting or a call-centre team answering customer queries. In this chapter, we'll talk about persuading an audience; but the skills of persuasion apply just as much when your audience is just one person.

Character (ethos)

We tend to believe people we believe to be 'of good character' – people we trust or respect. *Ethos* is the skill of establishing that trust and fostering that respect. If you want to develop your *ethos*, ask: *Why should my audience believe* me?

Aristotle suggested that ethos itself comprises three skills.

First, demonstrate that you share your audience's values. If you can show that your beliefs, priorities and attitudes align to those of your audience, they'll feel that you're one of them.

Secondly, display practical common sense. The Greeks called common sense *phronesis* and distinguished it from *sophia*, which is philosophical wisdom. You'll gain authority with your audience if you display moderation, rather than being dangerously radical or extreme in your views. Indicate that you know something about how the real world operates, and that textbook solutions don't always work out in practice. Favour the middle way.

And thirdly, demonstrate that you've invested personally in the idea you're arguing for. What have you done to contribute to making this proposition successful? Better still, what have you sacrificed?

All of these qualities are invested in you by your audience. Telling your audience that you share their values is not enough; you must demonstrate that you do so. What is moderate to one group may be unacceptably revolutionary to another. And if the audience has no interest in the cause to which you are committing, your *ethos* will suffer.

Demonstrate that you share your audience's values by giving examples. If you speak about a topic in abstract terms, your audience has no compelling reason to listen, because it's hard to pattern-match to abstract ideas. But if you begin with an example drawn from your own experience, they'll immediately listen with a more intense and sustained attention.

For example, rather than paying attention to the abstract idea of pragmatism, tell a story about how you solved a problem by adapting the rules to the circumstances. Or explain how you gained practical wisdom by making a mistake (and how you put things right). That candour, sincerity and vulnerability will do much to enhance your *ethos*.

Similarly with commitment. You might say that you're committed to delivering your work on time. It's the kind of anything anyone might say. But if you explain how you worked deep into the night on one occasion to get a proposal to the client by the agreed deadline, you've demonstrated that commitment, and given substance to your idea.

Next time you're preparing to make a case to a manager or team, put the argument to one side briefly, and note down how you can increase your ethos with whoever you're seeking to persuade. How can you demonstrate that you share their values? How can you demonstrate practical good sense and moderation? How can you demonstrate a sense of personal commitment to your proposal?

Logic (logos)

Logic would seem to be a supremely rational, conscious activity, compared with unconscious influence. By using *logos*, we're appealing to our audience's ability to reason. We construct an argument by making a case, and creating reasons to support that case. Reasons are linked to the case by logic.

But logic never works in conscious isolation. Every argument is based on assumptions, and those assumptions – by definition – are unconscious. If your argument is based on assumptions that your audience doesn't share, then no amount of logical argumentation will succeed in persuading them. (More about logic later in this chapter.)

Passion (pathos)

Pathos is usually defined as an appeal to the emotions. Every time we understand something by pattern-matching, the match will carry an emotional tag. The emotion might not be strong, but it will be immediate and it will always be simple: good or bad, like or dislike, trust or distrust. We apply these emotional tags to all the information we understand.

The function of any emotion is to tell us what to do. Specifically, emotions provoke us to act without needing to think: that's why we say that we feel moved when in the grip of an emotion. (Indeed, the very word 'emotion' contains the word 'motion'.) So, particularly if we want to persuade our audience to do something, we must engage their feelings. It may feel manipulative or dishonest; but if we ignore the pathetic appeal, our argument will fail to connect fully. (Mr Spock on Star Trek continually had this problem when trying to persuade his colleagues to act rationally.) Our rhetorical aim must be to stimulate the feeling appropriate to the action we want our audience to take.

Stimulating emotion, however, is not the same as telling the audience what to feel. Using emotional language, for example – adjectives like 'amazing', 'infuriating', 'delightful' or 'incredible' –

will almost always be counterproductive. We guard our emotional lives jealously; being told what emotion to feel is likely to trigger a defence mechanism. ('Why should I feel angry?') Instead, give an example or tell a story and let the audience supply the emotion. That's how *pathos* works.

Six principles of influence

Professor Robert Cialdini, in his bestseller *Influence: The Science of Persuasion*, identifies six patterns of influence, all of which operate unconsciously. Any one of them can enhance the pathetic appeal.

Reciprocity: the old give and take (and take)

We feel a strong urge to repay a favour. Offer your audience a gift – or a concession – and they may feel moved to do what you want.

Authority: directed deference

We're easily moved by people whose authority we recognize. (Here, *pathos* meets *ethos*.)

Scarcity: less is more

We're motivated to reach for something we think is in short supply. We're also motivated more by the prospect of losing something than gaining something. Point out what your audience might lose and you'll strike an emotional chord.

Consistency: I am what I say

We want to be seen to be consistent with past behaviours. Show that what you want someone to do aligns with something they have done or said in the past.

Alignment: truths are us

We're strongly influenced to feel and do what we know people around us are feeling and doing. Persuading people as a group can often be more successful than seeking to persuade them individually.

> **Liking: I like you, you're like me**
>
> We'd all prefer to say 'yes' to someone we know and like. Exploit your similarity to your audience: in your actions, in your words, even perhaps in the way you dress.
>
> (Remember these six patterns with the mnemonic RASCAL.)

Pathos can also awaken the imagination. We can think of imagination as the brain's 'reality generator': it draws on memories and visualizes possible futures, often by combining pattern-matches from different or even seemingly unrelated aspects of our experience.

In fact, imagination can temper emotion. It can focus your audience's attention *away* from an immediate emotional response and stimulate them to think about your argument more objectively and creatively: to see the potential in the situation and envisage the future you want to create. Imagination can allow your audience to become co-creators of your argument.

Finally, *pathos* seeks to create a sense of identification in your audience. You are trying to persuade them to identify with your argument (as co-creators); with you as the speaker (*pathos* links here with *ethos*); and with themselves. The pathetic appeal can weld your audience – at least for the moment in which you're persuading them – into a community of feeling and thinking.

A neat way to pull all this together is to tell a story. Biljana Scott, in a paper for the organization Diplo, says:

The Greek concept of pathos, *although defined as 'the appeal to emotion for rhetorical effect', tends to include within its remit imagination and a sense of fellow suffering (*pathos *means both 'suffering' and 'experience'); all defining components of a gripping story.*

Indeed, as we'll see in the next chapter, stories can encapsulate all three of Aristotle's persuasive appeals – *ethos*, *logos* and *pathos* – in one compelling package.

What's the big idea?

What do you want to say? A single idea is more likely to persuade your listener than a group of ideas, simply because one strong idea is easier to remember.

Take time to find that Big Idea. Conduct imaginary conversations in your head and note down the kind of things you might say. Now ask three questions:

- **'What is my objective?'** What do I want to achieve? What would I like to see happen?

- **'Who am I talking to?'** Why am I talking to this person about this objective? What do they already know? What more do they need to know? What do I want them to do? What ideas are likely to convince them?

- **'What is the most important thing I have to say to them?'** If I were only allowed a few minutes with them, what would I say? What if you had only a few seconds to get your Big Idea across? (Film executives call this 'the elevator pitch'. Imagine that you were in the lift with your listener for a few seconds between floors.)

Top tip

Write down your Big Idea as a single sentence. Read it out aloud. Does this sentence express what you want to say clearly and coherently? Now learn it by heart!

Now test your Big Idea. If you were to speak this sentence to your listener, would they ask you a question? If you're arguing a point, you're looking for the question 'Why?' Does your Big Idea provoke that question?

Arranging your ideas logically

Logic is the glue that binds ideas into arguments. In its most basic form, an argument consists of three elements:

- a claim (the point you're arguing for);
- a reason (a statement that supports the claim);
- and the word 'because'.

All the logic in your argument is tied up in that simple word: *because*.

Look back at your Big Idea. In logical terms, that is your claim. It should provoke the question 'Why?' in your audience. Your task is to find an answer – or a group of answers – to that question. You're looking for reasons to support the claim.

For example, if your Big Idea is *We should invest in system X*, one reason might be: *System X is the most effective system of its kind*. Most business arguments are best supported by a group of reasons, addressing all the key factors that an audience of executives might consider. So you might add other reasons to support your claim:

System X is the most effective system of its kind.
System X is cheaper than its competitors.
System X will integrate well with our existing systems.

Constructing an argument in this way – as a pyramid, with the claim at the top and a small group of supporting reasons – is a great way to present arguments in management. Presenting your Big Idea first and then supporting it will always work well when you're trying to persuade busy people.

Finding the warrant

Every argument is based on assumptions. Surfacing and testing those assumptions is a critical step in constructing a persuasive argument.

Let's take a very simple argument and analyse it. If you say 'Eat more vegetables because they're good for you,' the statement before 'because' is your claim, and the statement after it is your reason.

How persuasive is this argument? It depends who you're trying to persuade.

In any argument, the connection between claim and reason here is based on an assumption. If we agree with the assumption that we should always do what's good for our health, then we're likely to accept the argument that we should eat more vegetables. A medical student, for example, might accept the assumption but then demand evidence that vegetables are indeed good for us. A child, in contrast, is unlikely to share the assumption that we should always do what's good for us – and with them, the argument is likely to fail.

This underlying assumption, connecting the reason to the claim, is sometimes called a warrant. If your listener shares the warrant underlying your argument, you have a good chance of persuading them. But if they don't share that assumption, the argument could fail. Indeed, many sound arguments fail – in the home, in the media, and in the workplace – because the audience doesn't share the warrant that underlies them. We see this mismatch most vividly in political or religious arguments, but you'll spot it also in business meetings, interviews and sales conversations. If you're arguing a case, pay close attention to the assumptions that underlie it. Does your audience share those assumptions?

Expressing your ideas

When we express our ideas, we need to combine the rational *logos* of our argument with the emotional and imaginative appeal of *pathos*. Pictures may work better than words: if you want your audience to donate to an animal charity, show them a picture of an animal in distress (better still, bring an animal on stage with you). The appeal to the senses isn't restricted to visual images, of course;

think about how any of the five senses might respond to your Big Idea.

Examples

Perhaps the simplest way to bring an idea alive is to offer a concrete example. Audiences can pattern-match far more easily to a single example than to a mass of statistics. A good example will also show that you know your stuff, and that you can apply it to real life (a key element of *ethos*.) Find an instance where the idea has been put into practice, or where it has created real results – either useful or disastrous.

Convincing examples have three key characteristics:

- First, they usually include real people doing real things. Can you give an example of someone doing something that illustrates your Big Idea?

- Secondly, they include vivid description, which stimulates one or more of the five senses. What does this example sound like, look like, feel or taste like?

- And thirdly, convincing examples involve feeling or emotion. Talk about how pleased the client was, how relieved you were, how excited you are by this idea.

Using metaphors

As we saw towards the end of Chapter 3, metaphors express one thing in terms of another. By linking a topic to something the listener already knows about, you create a pattern-matching bridge that allows them to cross over into your thinking.

You can also extend the metaphor to explain a more complicated or unusual topic. Think carefully about the metaphor you choose. For example, Dana Meadows, one of the gurus of systems theory, explains feedback loops using the metaphor of filling a glass with water. You turn on the tap; you watch the water level rise, and as it nears the top of the glass you regulate the flow of water. When the glass is full, you turn off the tap. We can extend the metaphor to help us think more widely about feedback loops. For example, if you can't see the glass, or if the flow of water is too fast, you'll find operating the feedback loop more difficult.

To find the right metaphor, start with your audience:

- What do you know about what they know?
- What do you want them to be able to do as a result of understanding the topic?
- What aspects of your topic do you want to explain?
- What else in the world shares the qualities you're trying to explain?
- Experiment with the metaphor and see how far you can extend it.
- Review your choice. Are you making the topic easier to understand?

Remembering your ideas

In the days before printing, memory played a vital role in the art of rhetoric. With no ready means of making notes or easy access to books, orators had to remember what to say, and in what order. Whole systems of memory were invented to help them.

These days, the art of memory has been replaced by technology – except, perhaps, for passing examinations. We have no need to remember: merely to read and store e-mails, pick up messages on the mobile, plug in, surf and download...

But memory still plays an important part in persuading others. You will persuade more effectively if you're not reciting from a sheaf of notes. Find a way to bring the ideas off paper and into your head. Give yourself some clear mental signposts so that you can find your way from one idea to the next. Have a way of showing your thoughts as you explain them: a notepad, a flip chart, a whiteboard.

Exercise

Next time you're preparing an argument, find time to draw a picture of it. Put all your notes away: you're working from memory here. Find as large a piece of paper as possible, and pens or pencils of different colours, and draw the argument as a journey, or perhaps a storyboard (like a strip cartoon, the kind of drawings film-makers use to map out a sequence of shots). You're aiming for a single route through the material. Put memorable stopping places along the way: signposts, buildings, statues, posters... Now use your drawing to help you rehearse.

Delivering effectively

You are as much a part of the persuasive process as your argument. (*Ethos* supports *logos*.) If you're saying one thing but your body is saying another, no one will believe your words.

Start, as ever, with the audience you're trying to persuade. Do they favour a relaxed, informal conversational style, or a more formal, presentational delivery? Are they interested in the broad picture or lots of supporting detail? Will they want to ask questions?

We have three sets of resources to help us deliver our argument. Think about the way you use your:

- eyes;
- voice;
- body.

Effective eye contact

We speak more with our eyes than with our voices. Maintain eye contact with your listener. If you're talking to more than one person, include everybody with your eyes. Focus on their eyes: don't look through them.

Using your voice

Your voice will sound more persuasive if it's not too high, too fast or too thin. Regulate and strengthen your breathing while you speak. Breathe deep and slow. Let your voice emerge more from your body than from your throat. The more body your voice has, and the more measured your vocal delivery, the more convincing you'll sound.

You'll find more tips on breathing in Chapter 7. Meanwhile, try this exercise.

Exercise

Here's how to find the best version of your voice. (Thanks to Caroline Goyder for this exercise.) Put your thumb just below where your ribs separate (just below where the front of a bra strap goes – if you wear one). You're feeling for a layer of muscle: massage it gently and feel it soften. Now gently tap that point and let out a big belly laugh. Or yawn loudly. Feel how the sound of your voice drops down and becomes more relaxed. Jump up and down and speak. Become aware of how your voice is coming from your centre – almost up from your lower spine. That's the voice you're looking for. Everyone has it; we just need to find it. Once you've done this exercise, try singing what you want to say. Listen to how your voice shifts between speaking and singing. You're aiming to locate the source of your voice between your chest and your stomach – not your throat.

Persuasive body language

Your face, your limbs and your body posture will all contribute to the total persuasive effect. Keep your facial muscles moving and your neck muscles relaxed. Use your hands to paint pictures, to help you find the right words and express yourself fully. Don't sit back or close your body off when you're seeking to persuade; don't hide behind a desk or a lectern. Bring yourself forward, open yourself up and present yourself, along with your ideas.

Summary points

- The three modes of persuasion are:
  - ethos: appealing to our audience's sense of our character or reputation;
  - logos: appealing to their reason;
  - pathos: appealing to their emotions.
- Ethos is the appeal to our audience through:
  - shared values;
  - moderation;
  - commitment to a cause.

    Logos appeals to reason.

    Pathos appeals to emotion and to the imagination.

    Find your Big Idea by asking:
  - What is my objective?
  - Who am I talking to?
  - What is the most important thing I have to say to them?

- Find reasons to answer the question 'Why?'
- Use the pyramid principle to organize your argument: Big Idea first, supported by reasons.
- Arrange the argument by placing your Big Idea first, and supporting it with reasons.
- Identify the warrant that supports your argument and check that your audience shares that warrant.
- To express your ideas more vividly, use:
  - images;
  - examples;
  - metaphors.
- To remember your material, use visual aids such as:
  - mind maps;
  - flipcharts;
  - whiteboards.
- And to deliver your ideas well:
  - maintain effective eye contact;
  - use your voice well;
  - make your body language persuasive.

06
Storytelling and the uses of narrative

As the twentieth century slipped into the twenty-first, corporate storytelling started to become big business. In 2011, for example, no more than 5,000 marketing professionals listed storytelling as a key skill on LinkedIn. By 2017, the number had risen to 570,000.

Why this sudden surge of interest? People at work were facing an information explosion, and the traditional methods of communication were struggling to make their mark. Presentations built around busy PowerPoint slides, official policy statements and excitable announcements from the internal comms department were routinely greeted with cynicism, and often ignored.

Stories seemed to offer a way to cut through the complexity. Researchers suggested that we're more likely to remember a story than a set of statistics. And, indeed, leaders have understood the power of stories for thousands of years. Political leaders use stories to gain loyalty and legitimize their rule. Community leaders use stories to create a sense of group identity. Military leaders tell stories to reduce fear and boost morale. Religious leaders use stories to reinforce belief and teach life lessons.

Business leaders, in contrast, often resisted the challenge to tell stories. They were nervously aware that many of the stories being told in their organizations were subversive or downright destructive.

Yet gossip, rumour and the bush telegraph undeniably achieve shared understanding more effectively and efficiently than the most carefully crafted mission statement.

How, then, can we use stories productively?

What is a story?

A story is a form of conversation. It requires a storyteller and an audience. The storyteller relates a sequence of events – usually called a narrative – in which characters do things to change an initial situation. The audience contributes to the story by reacting to events as they unfold, by participating vicariously in the action, and by commenting on the narrative. They may even applaud at the end of the story.

An effective story has four key features.

Stories have characters

One of the characters might be us. And, of course, we can include other people in the story. But a character doesn't have to be human. It could be the deer that ran out in front of our car last night; or the computer that crashed just when we were rushing to complete a vital paper; or the bread that failed to rise in the oven.

The characters are always doing something

They're interacting with their situation, their environment, or with other characters. And the narrator will assemble those actions into a coherent narrative sequence.

A story always includes a moment of tension

There is a turning point, a 'hinge' around which the story revolves. The main character – the protagonist or hero – encounters a problem and has to solve it; perhaps they have to make a critical choice.

The conclusion of the story generates social meaning

A story without a moral will leave us dissatisfied. This 'so what' element is the reason for telling the story in the first place.

Gossip contains all four of these elements. If you tell me about something that happened to you on the bus this morning, it will have all those key elements:

- characters;
- events, set out in a narrative sequence;
- a moment of tension: choice, conflict, an obstacle to be overcome;
- resolution and meaning.

Most gossip is about other people. The story often focuses on the actions of an absent character: someone other than the narrator or the audience. The story usually highlights behaviour that is anti-social or unacceptable. Gossip thus serves to create social bonds, in part by identifying and shaming people who flout those bonds. You're not just telling me what the absent person did; you're telling me what those actions mean to you. And you're inviting me to feel the same. Stories thus cement relationships between individuals, and within groups. They help us reinforce social values.

Indeed, we share a huge amount of knowledge as stories, from personal life events to jokes, from rumours to urban myths. We tell stories to reinforce our communal identity and explain complicated events. We consume stories avidly in the form of novels, news, movies and soap operas. There's clearly something about stories that fulfils a very deep human need.

Exercise

Analyse a story you told today. Pick a simple example. Identify the four key elements in the story:

- Who were the characters?
- What were the key events in the narrative sequence?
- What was the point of maximum tension – the 'hinge' in the story?
- What point is the story making?
- How well did you tell the story? How much did you prepare? (Perhaps you reconstructed or assembled the elements of the story, and rehearsed it in your mind before delivering it.)
- How easy was the process of creating this little story?

How stories work

How do stories work their magic?

First, they lock our attention. The human mind has a natural tendency to wander and day-dream. A story latches on to that fantasizing tendency and channels it. Absorbed in a good book, or a box-set, our minds become calm and pay close, steady attention, often for hours on end. We go into a kind of trance state, which helps us embed information – including quite complicated information – deep in our memories ready for use in the future.

Secondly, stories create a powerful sense of empathy. Research using fMRI machines shows that, when we are engaged with a story, our brains operate as if we're participating in the story ourselves. When the hero looks angry, the viewer's brain displays the tell-tale signs of anger. If a character weeps, we're likely to do the same. And we seem to find this fellow-feeling intensely pleasurable: we even submit willingly to feelings of horror or terror in pursuit of this experience of intense empathy.

Finally, stories help us learn. They simulate experiences without us having to live through them. By showing how a character overcomes a barrier, confronts an enemy or solves a problem, the story helps us imagine how *we* might solve the same problem – without taking the risks that the hero takes. In this sense, stories act a little like play: they stimulate our imagination to generate new ways of looking at reality and new ways of interacting with it.

The magic of storytelling operates socially. All three of these effects – the close, trance-like attention, the sense of identification, the achieved learning – occur not just in individuals, but in groups. Stories have been described as 'adaptive collective sense-making': in other words, stories create a truly shared understanding of reality.

This ability of stories to generate shared meaning makes them especially useful at times of sudden or unforeseen change for a community. Such situations – radical changes within an organization, natural disasters, sudden outbreaks of disease, aggression by external enemies – threaten our sense of social identity. A powerful story can re-establish the sense of shared meaning that reinforces the bonds within the group and helps it to survive and prosper.

How to tell a good story

How, then, can we add stories to our set of communication skills? How can we exploit the power of narrative to engage and influence people more effectively?

Exercise

You may be feeling that you have no stories to tell. It's a common feeling, especially if your work involves a good deal of analytical thinking. But the stories are there: people are telling them all the time. Some get told over and over again, and become part of an organization's culture. And some will be unhelpful (which is why so many managers fear the power of gossip).

But it's impossible to ban storytelling. People will tell stories about you and your organization, whether you want them to or not. Fortunately, you can help choose which stories they tell. How? By telling them first.

Start to collect your own stories. Pay attention. When something memorable happens – something you have learnt from, something that might help your colleagues learn – note it down. A great story is about to be born.

Here's a process for crafting a story, in three stages.

- Choose a message.
- Choose your characters.
- Choose a structure.

Each of these three choices is informed by the same question: the question we're asking ourselves whenever we communicate. *What effect am I having?*

Choose a message

We might call this our take-home message. It's the moral of the story: the idea we want our audience to accept at the end. The message of the story answers the question: *So what?* What is the significance of this story, not just for you but for your audience?

Begin by thinking about how you want to influence your audience's thoughts, feelings and actions. The most obviously useful stories are case studies, which offer practical examples of concepts or key ideas. Leaders are often recommended to use a story to help set a vision for the organization, to define its culture and values, or to help people navigate change.

Exercise

Here are three useful questions to ask as you begin to plan your story.

1. What do I want my audience to think?

What do you want the audience to know by the end? How do you want them to think differently about the topic? What's the 'aha' or the 'so what' – the major shift in their thinking you're looking for?

2. What do I want my audience to feel?

What emotion or response do you want to evoke? What feeling do you most want to associate with your topic? Do you want people to feel hopeful? Angry? Provoked? Confident? Scared? Do you want them to feel motivated, energized or inspired? Presumably you want them to feel entertained throughout – and not baffled or bored.

3. What do I want my audience to do?

What action do you want the audience to take? Do you want them to change their lifestyle? Is there a specific 'to-do' or next step? Is there something they need to change? The best calls to action are clear and simple.

Next, find the topic of your story. You presumably know what your story will be about. Call this the story's subject: 'customer service', maybe. The word topic comes from the Greek word *topos*, meaning 'place'. The topic of the story is your position on the subject: your point of view, what a journalist might call your 'angle' on the subject.

A quick and easy way to identify a topic is to create a phrase beginning with the word 'how'. For example, if our subject is customer service, we might choose:

How one distribution centre re-invented the concept of customer service.

Now simply find the sentence that expresses the 'so what?' implied by your topic. In this example, the message might be:

We can all re-invent the concept of customer service – and here's how.

Choose your characters

A narrative becomes a story when it acquires characters. Many stories focus on a protagonist, often called the Hero. We identify with the Hero; their struggles with choice, or difficulty, or obstacles, help us inhabit the story and relate to it.

The Hero could be you. Business leaders are often advised, in speeches to their staff, to tell a personal story: a life event that reveals some vulnerable aspect of themselves, which might seem more authentic to an audience than presenting a series of strategic objectives. And, indeed, if your story is suitably dramatic, full of challenges overcome and dragons slain, then your audience might be happy to see you as the Hero. Choose the story carefully: how does it increase your credibility? Think back to the skills of *ethos* we explored in the previous chapter: sharing your audience's values; demonstrating practical good sense and moderation; showing commitment to the cause. How will your story illustrate those persuasive elements?

In fact, the best way to establish your authority as the storyteller may be to elevate another character to the status of Hero. In our customer service example, the Hero could be a team member who suggested an innovative way of delivering better service, and then faced a number of challenges in getting their idea accepted (thus generating suspense and tension). Imagine how your audience could identify with this character and find inspiration in their struggle.

But there's a third possibility. The Hero could be your audience. This is a particularly good idea if you want to influence policy makers or decision makers.

Imagine, for example, that you're asking for funds from a grant committee or a funding organization. What do *they* want? How do they want to be seen? How could your story help them? Making them the Hero of the story might help them feel that they're making the right choice in giving you money. You, the storyteller, are merely helping them achieve their goal. They are Luke Skywalker, as it were, and you are Obi Wan Kenobi: the Wise Guide or Mentor, who can help them overcome the perils of the Hero's journey and win the treasure.

And then there may be other characters in your story. Who is the Villain? Who is the helpless Victim? In our customer service example, the Villain might be a competitor who is undercutting on service costs but compromising quality; the Victims, of course, might be your customers.

Choose a structure

Your topic will often give you a strong clue about the shape of your story. That shape will always be linear: it will have a beginning, a middle and an end. You, the narrator, are taking your audience on a journey. Does the journey take us to a new place? Or does it leave home and return home? In our example, the journey involved in re-inventing customer service itself implies a powerful narrative.

Storytellers often talk about the narrative arc. The arc describes the way the story moves from beginning to end. It's an arc because it rises to a point of maximum tension – the 'hinge' that we discussed earlier in this chapter – and then resolves that tension. This moment of maximum tension is the most important point in the narrative arc; resolving it generates the meaning or significance of the story. (A cliff-hanger, of course, plays with this structure by leaving the audience at a point of maximum tension and forcing them to wait before resolving it.)

Here's a simple four-part structure that you can use to construct your narrative. I remember it by using the letters SPQR (which is the motto of the Roman Empire).

Situation

Think of this as 'Once upon a time...' You're setting the scene. Where is the story located? When did it happen?

Problem

Something happens to complicate the Situation. Tension causes the narrative arc to rise. Surprising and unexpected Problems are more likely to hook your audience's attention. Perhaps something goes wrong, or something is lost. Perhaps the Hero is called to pursue a quest (the Quest is often a key component of the Hero's Journey). Perhaps the Villain seeks to frustrate the Hero's ambitions. As you explore this stage of the narrative structure, look for opportunities to create suspense. Stories that set up problems but withhold the solutions will be far more compelling.

Question

This is the point of maximum tension. The Hero faces a seemingly insuperable difficulty: how will they overcome it? How will they escape or meet the challenge? The Question might be one of choice: which solution to pick, which road to take? The Question is the 'hinge' around which the story revolves.

Response (or Resolution)

The actions of the Hero answer the Question. The Response also acts as a Resolution of the Problem. Tension is released; the narrative arc now dips towards its final resting point. The Hero has reached the end of the journey; perhaps they return home, sadder and wiser. And the world has changed. The Response or Resolution supplies the all-important 'so what?' element that gives the whole story its meaning.

A narrative arc might contain smaller ones within it. For example, the Hero's journey might include a series of challenges, each its own arc.

Narrative arcs can vary in shape. But these variations play on the same basic idea: the build-up towards a point of maximum tension and the resolution of that tension.

Exercise: Finding the plot

The variations on the narrative arc generate different kinds of plot. Some writers have suggested that there are a finite number of plots, which stories replicate over and over again. Here, for instance, are three plots that you may recognize from different stories, novels or movies that you've enjoyed. One of these plots might form the basis of your own story.

The Challenge Plot: a protagonist overcomes a formidable challenge and succeeds.

The Connection Plot: people develop a relationship that bridges a gap, racial, class, ethnic, religious, demographic, or otherwise.

The Creativity Plot: someone makes a mental breakthrough, solves a long-standing puzzle, or attacks a problem in an innovative way.

Using narrative to explain

Narrative provides the underlying structure of a good story. But we can also use that same structure to communicate in other ways. Most communication at work involves explaining or persuading, and narrative can help us do both.

Have you ever found yourself trying to explain something and failing? What seems transparently clear to you remains stubbornly incomprehensible to the other person. The reason may be that your explanation – however clear it is – is not creating pattern-matches in your listener's mind.

We explain in different ways – specifically, in six different ways. These six patterns help us to explain clearly. Some patterns are relatively easy to understand: listing examples, for instance (who doesn't love a bullet list?), or setting out a process in numbered steps (instructions, for instance, or a well written recipe). Other patterns require a bit more careful thinking: grouping items into categories; comparing or contrasting two things; defining something clearly. But one pattern of explanation seems to stand out from all the rest as uniquely powerful. And the reason seems to have something to do with its connection to narrative.

Human beings love to explain reality in terms of cause and effect. Toddlers learn early that if they drop an object from their high chair, it will fall to the floor. Later, we learn that if we flick a switch, the lights come on. We nearly always ignore the technical process by which this happens; we simply remember that one action causes the other. More generally, if we witness two events in sequence, we will tend to assume that the first event has caused the second. And if we listen to, or read, two statements, we will assume that the first links to the second in some way by cause and effect.

Our preference for explanations by cause and effect is a feature of the systemizing drive that we explored in Chapter 2, which gives us a sense of control over our environment. It comes into play particularly strongly when we feel that sense of control being frustrated. If we flick the switch and the lights fail to come on, we look for the cause. We may even unconsciously assume that some conscious agent made the second event happen deliberately. We might, for instance, say that the car 'refused' to start one cold morning; that a stock price 'struggled' to reach a certain level; or that a disease is 'resisting' treatment. The principle seems to be:

When we can't find a cause, assume personal intent.

Causality and intention are the key drivers of every good story. So, if you want to explain something clearly – especially to a non-expert – look for a pattern of cause and effect. Key elements of your explanation could act as characters: a machine, for instance, or an app; even a molecule or a chemical compound. Perhaps you can illustrate an abstract concept by translating it into human action: a complex financial concept, for example, played out by investors or bankers buying and selling. In other words, find the story.

Using narrative to persuade

In the previous chapter, we saw how we can persuade in three ways: the logic of an argument needs to be supported by *ethos* and *pathos*. We can create this support in part by preparing our audience for the argument's Big Idea: to focus their attention, fill them in on the background, or set the context. And a neat way to pull all this together can be to use narrative.

Let's go back to the SPQR structure we explored earlier.

Situation

Briefly tell your audience something they already know. Your Situation statement might begin at some point in the past ('When we started this company, ten years ago...'); it might begin with a statement of shared beliefs ('We all know that...'; 'Everyone here recognizes that...'). You're showing that you understand their situation and can appreciate their point of view. (That's *ethos* at work.) You're also showing that you identify with them. (There's the touch of *pathos*.)

Problem

Now identify a Problem that has arisen within the Situation. The Problem complicates the Situation in some way. Something may have gone wrong, or be threatening to go wrong. Something may have changed (or not changed). We may not know what to do; we may be facing a range of options from which we must choose. Unlike the Situation, the Problem will probably be new information for your audience. And it should make them pay attention. This is something they need to know about. It really should be their Problem.

Don't forget the *pathos* at this point. Negative problems might arouse fear or concern; opportunities should arouse a sense of excitement. Don't sidestep these emotions. Acknowledge the feelings aroused by the Problem.

Question

The Problem should prompt your audience to ask a Question. Presumably, you want them to ask the Question that allows you to deliver your Big Idea. Tell the story to maximize your chances that your audience asks that very Question.

Situation	Problem	Question
Stable, agreed status quo	Something's gone wrong.	What do we do?
	Something could go wrong.	How do we stop it?
		How do we adjust to it?
	Something's changed.	How do we prepare for it?
	Something could change.	What can we do?
	Something new has arisen.	Who's right?
		What do we do?
	Someone has a different point of view.	How do we choose?
	We don't know what to do.	Which course do we take?
	There are a number of things we could do.	

Response

Your Response to the Question should be your Big Idea. Your audience should now be ready to consider that idea because it answers a question that they have asked.

SPQR is a great narrative framework for introducing an argument. Management consultants often use it to structure the introductions of their proposals. The trick is to tell the story quickly. Don't be tempted to fill out the story with lots of detail.

We can also use narrative to construct, not just the introduction to an argument, but the argument itself. And doing so is particularly useful when we're making a presentation – as we'll see in the next chapter.

Summary points

- A story is a form of conversation. It has four key features:
  - stories have characters;
  - the characters are always doing something;
  - a story always includes a moment of tension;
  - the conclusion of the story generates social meaning.
- Stories are effective because they:
  - engage our attention;
  - create a sense of empathy and participation; and
  - help us learn.
- Above all, stories are social: they create a shared understanding of reality.
  To tell a good story:
  - choose a message;
  - choose your characters;
  - choose a structure;
- Ask what you want your audience to:
  - think;
  - feel;
  - do.

- Establish your story's subject, topic and message.
    Identify the characters in the story: especially the Hero.
    Map out the story's narrative arc:

    - Situation;

    - Problem;

    - Question;

    - Response or Resolution.

- We can use narrative structures to help explain: build your explanation around patterns of cause and effect.
    We can also use narrative to help us persuade: in part, by introducing an argument with a narrative structure outlining its background or context (SPQR again).

07
Making a presentation

Think of a presentation as a formal conversation. It's a largely one-way conversation with a few specific rules: you are speaking, and the audience is supposed to be listening. You're leading; they are following. It's not the most natural of conversations. And that is where the challenges begin.

Top tip

Many people now use the word 'presentation' to refer to a slide deck – indeed, for many people, the slides *are* the presentation. There are notes on producing slides later in this chapter, but your presentation is *not* the slides. The presentation is *you*, engaging your audience's attention.

A recent study in the United States asked people about their deepest fears. Intriguingly, death came in at number seven. At the top of the list – above deep water, financial problems, insects and heights – was speaking to groups.

Why the anxiety? I think it's because, when we present, we put ourselves on show. The audience will be judging not just our ideas, but *us*. People may not easily remember reports or spreadsheets; but they will certainly remember a presenter who looks nervous or incompetent.

That nervous, jittery feeling is caused by adrenalin, a hormone secreted by your adrenal glands (near your kidneys). Adrenalin constricts your arteries, increasing your blood pressure and stimulating the heart. Why stimulate the heart? To give you extra energy. And when do you need extra energy? When you're in danger.

Adrenalin release is an evolved response to threat. It's all part of the fight-or-flight response, which helps us to confront or run away from life-threatening situations. Symptoms include a rapid pulse (to keep the blood well oxygenated), dilated pupils (so that we can see better) and sweaty palms (to help us grip a weapon).

That adrenalin rush has two other effects. It increases your concentration – particularly useful when making a presentation. Less usefully, adrenalin also stimulates excretion of body waste. This decreases your body weight, helping you to run faster. And *that* is why you want to visit the toilet immediately before presenting.

But the worst of it is that the audience will forget virtually everything you say.

That's the bad news.

The good news is that nervousness can help you to present more effectively. It's telling you that this presentation matters – and that *you* matter. An effective presenter puts themselves centre-stage; so you have every right to feel nervous. In fact, you *should* feel nervous. Your task is to *manage* those nerves.

Exercise

The best way to deal with nerves is to work on your breathing. Find somewhere comfortable to sit and relax. Relax your shoulders and put your hands on your stomach. Breathe in and out, if you can, through your nose: breathe in for a count of seven and out for a count of eleven. If these counts are too high, start

with lower numbers – 3/6 perhaps – and work up towards 7/11.
The important thing is to breathe *out* for longer than you breathe
in. Check your shoulders: they should be remaining still. Check
your hands: they should be gently pushing your stomach *out* as
you breathe in, and falling back into your stomach as you breathe
out. It may help to close your eyes and concentrate on counting
as you do this exercise. (Combine this with the exercise on using
your voice in Chapter 5.)

Steady breathing – to a rhythm of 7 beats in and 11 beats out – is
brilliant for calming nerves and reducing anxiety. Breathing in
quickens the heartbeat and stimulates adrenalin production;
breathing out does the opposite, slowing the heart and the
production of adrenalin. We tend to breathe in too much when we
are anxious; 7/11 breathing simply reverses the connection, so that
our breathing makes us less anxious.

Preparing for the presentation

Those nerves also reflect the uncertainty of a live presentation. The
Greeks called this element *kairos*, a word that translates roughly as
'the opportune moment'.

The effective presenter understands that their presentation will
be affected by a host of uncontrollable factors. You can't plan for
the audience's mood. You may not even be able to foresee who will
be there. You can't plan for any sudden external development that
might affect your topic. You can't plan for every question that you
might be asked.

But that, of course, is also the greatest strength of a presentation.
You and the audience are together, in the same place, at the same
time. This is a unique moment. You can respond to the *kairos*, if, as
the Greeks did, you see it as an opportunity.

Exercise

What will affect the *kairos* the next time you make a presentation? Spend a little time thinking about the specific circumstances you will be working with: the audience's mood, what has been happening to them recently, events in the outside world that will be on their minds. How can you adapt your presentation to acknowledge or address those factors?

If you can support your nerves with solid preparation, you can channel your nervous energy into the performance itself. Prepare in three areas:

- the material;
- the audience;
- yourself.

Managing the material

Your most important task is to hold the audience's attention.

Presentations fail for many reasons. Perhaps the most common problem is that the presenter talks *about* something, rather than talking *to the audience*.

Other presentations fail because the presenter organizes the material as if it's a document. A presentation is not a report – or a set of slides. It needs to be structured as a *narrative*. Your presentation must take the audience on a journey, with lots of interesting twists and turns along the way to hold their attention. All the skills of storytelling and narrative that we explored in Chapter 6 will be useful in planning your material.

Defining your objective

Why are you presenting? What do you want your audience to *do* at the end?

Presentations are ideal for *influencing* and *persuading* an audience. On the whole, a presentation is not a good medium for *explaining* something. It's worth repeating this point: your audience is probably going to forget almost everything you say. So packing your presentation full of information – on slides, or anywhere else – will be counterproductive. If your brief is to explain something, try to find some persuasive element that will inject passion and purpose into the presentation. And if you *must* offer your audience detailed information, put it in supporting notes.

I believe that there's only one reason why you should be making a presentation. It may sound rather grand, but a presentation should *inspire* your audience. Think back to all the elements of *pathos* that we explored in Chapter 5. Your audience wants to be moved, intrigued, and involved. Above all, they want to feel that they can *identify* with you and your ideas. They also want to identify with each other: that they are, for the brief time that this presentation lasts, a single community. Your task is to create in your audience that multiple sense of identification – with you, with your ideas and with themselves – so that they'll be inspired to act.

Write down your objective in one sentence. This helps you to:

- clear your mind;
- select material to fit;
- check at the end of planning that you are still addressing a single clear issue.

Write a simple sentence beginning:

'The aim of this presentation is to…'

Make sure the verb following that word 'to' is suitably inspirational!

Analysing your audience

Your presentation will be successful if the audience feels that you have spoken directly to them. If your ideas directly address their needs, they will pay much more attention to them. Remember the skills of *ethos*, which we also explored in Chapter 5? If you can show that you share the audience's values, that you value practical common sense and the middle way, and that you have made a personal investment in your ideas, your audience will respect you. And if they respect you, they'll be more inclined to believe you.

So think about your audience carefully.

- How many will there be?
- What is their status range?
- Will they want to be there?
- How much do they already know about the matter? How much more do they need to know?
- How does your message and your material relate to the audience?
- Is the audience young or old? Are they predominantly one gender or mixed?

Your audience has certain expectations – of you and of itself. They will expect you to be competent, to set the pace and direction of the presentation, and to stay in control. They will expect themselves to be led, to be told what to think and feel, and to respond as a single group. (They certainly won't want you to cause division, disagreements and bad feeling between themselves.)

Audiences can respond actively in presentations in only a few ways. They can interrupt you – to ask a question, to contradict you or to heckle you; they can laugh; and they can applaud. Your audience will expect you to manage these responses.

Constructing a message

Once you have your objective, and some sense of who your audience is, you can plan your material.

Work out your message. Look back at our notes on messages in Chapter 5. Your presentation's message must:

- be a sentence;
- express your objective;
- contain a single idea;
- have no more than 15 words;
- grab your audience's attention.

Make your message as vivid as you can. An effective take-home message sticks in the mind long after the presentation is over.

Top tip

The subject of your presentation matters far less than your message. People giving ordinary presentations *talk about* something: that's the subject. Brilliant presenters *say* something to their audience: that's the message, Focus, always, on your message.

Creating a structure

Everything in the structure of the presentation should revolve around your message.

You could use Aristotle's three modes of appeal as a structuring device (we looked at these at the start of Chapter 5).

- Start with *ethos*: establish your credentials for speaking to this audience.

- Continue with *logos*: deliver your message and a small number of supporting points (three is always a good number to aim for).

- And end with *pathos*: a rousing call to action that appeals to your audience's emotions.

If you have only a short time to plan your presentation, this three-part structure will serve you well. If you have longer to prepare, develop this structure into a narrative. Identify the problem that you want to address; identify the hero or heroes of the story; and think about how you can introduce surprise and suspense into the structure of your material. (All the ideas in Chapter 6 will help you.)

Monroe's motivated sequence

In the 1930s, Alan Monroe, a psychology professor at Purdue University in Indiana, invented a model that develops the three-part structure into a five-step narrative sequence. Monroe suggested that, 'when confronted with a problem, people look for a solution; when they feel a want or need, they search for a way to satisfy it'. Monroe's motivated sequence structures a presentation to exploit this desire to satisfy needs.

At step one, capture the audience's attention. Ask a question, tell a story or use a quotation. Above all, say or do something *surprising*. At this point, the audience should be asking itself: 'Where is this presentation going? What's going to happen?'

At step two, convince the audience that they're confronting a problem. They may already know about this problem; showing that you understand it will increase your *ethos* with them. Or you might present them with a new, shocking problem. Create dissatisfaction and discomfort, and the need for resolution.

At this point, the audience should be saying to itself: 'This is serious. What can we do?'

At step three, introduce your solution. How will it solve the problem? This is the heart of your presentation: it's where *logos* comes to the fore. Build a pyramid (we looked at pyramids in Chapter 5). Drive home your key message and lay out a small number of key points to support it. Summarize your ideas as you go, so that the audience never gets lost. At this point, they should be saying: 'This seems to be the obvious solution. But how will it work in practice? And how will it affect me?'

At step four, visualize the future. Invoke *pathos* by stimulating your audience's imagination. Describe how the world will look if the audience does nothing. Or describe a world in which your solution has been implemented. Or do both. At this point, the audience should be almost audibly crying out: 'Tell us what to do!'

Finally, at step five, make your call to action. Make the action simple and, if possible, immediate. And don't forget the *pathos*: we act on our emotions, so stir the audience with the emotion that's appropriate to the action you want them to take.

Monroe's motivated sequence has served presenters well for almost 90 years. It's adaptable to many different themes. Above all, it helps us to plan material that speaks directly to our audience, using a narrative structure.

Putting it on cards

The very best presenters work without notes. They speak with effortless ease, apparently improvising a seamless thread of glittering eloquence.

Don't be fooled. That spontaneity has been carefully planned and rehearsed. We could all aim for this ideal, but there's no shame in not quite achieving it. On the way to speaking without notes, you could consider writing the full text of your presentation, reading from an autocue (which displays the text you speak on a semi-transparent screen), or putting prompt notes onto cards. All three methods have advantages and challenges.

A script gives you complete control. You need never stumble over your words again! Using a script, you can choose your words carefully and time your presentation to the second. On the other hand, you may not be very competent at reading a script; the words may remain obstinately on the page and refuse to leap into life.

An autocue releases you from the burden of looking down to read your script. You can look up and around, while actually reading your script. And that might help to energize your delivery.

Most presenters choose the option of notes on cards. Filing or archive cards are best; use the largest you can find. Cards have a number of key advantages.

- They are less shaky than paper – they don't rustle.
- They are more compact.
- They give your hands something firm to hold.
- They look more professional.
- They force you to write only brief notes.

By writing only brief notes, triggers and cues on your cards, you force yourself to think about what you are saying, while you are saying it. As a result, you'll sound more convincing.

The challenge of using cards is that you'll have to think about what to say. You may hesitate; 'ums' and 'ers' may appear; you may find yourself using irritating mannerisms or meaningless phrases (some presenters don't even notice that they're using them until they're told by a kind colleague). To overcome these glitches in delivery, try to cultivate deliberate silence while you're working out what to say.

Write your notes in bold print, using pen or felt-tip. Write on only one side and number the cards sequentially. Include:

- what you *must* say;
- what you *should* say to support the main idea;
- what you *could* say if you have time.

Keep the cards simple to look at, and rehearse with them so that you get to know them. And don't forget to hold them together with a treasury tag!

> ## Exercise
>
> The next time you're preparing a presentation, find time to draw
> a picture of it. Put all your notes away; you are working from
> memory here. Find as large a piece of paper as possible, and
> pens or pencils of different colours, and draw the presentation
> as a journey, or perhaps a storyboard (like a strip cartoon, the
> kind of drawings that film-makers use to map out a sequence of
> shots). You're aiming for a single route through the material. Put
> memorable stopping places along the way: signposts, buildings,
> statues, posters, etc. Now use your drawing to help you rehearse.

PRAISE: Adding spice

Exciting presentations bring ideas alive. There's a famous story
about a little girl who claimed she liked plays on the radio, 'because
the pictures were better'. Pictures on slides can be good; but *these*
pictures – the ones you create in your audience's minds with your
words – are often far more effective.

Here are six ways in which you can stimulate your audience's
imagination. We can remember them using the mnemonic PRAISE.

- *Proverbs* state ideas in memorable form. Make your message or
  your key points sound like advertising jingles or political
  slogans. Your audience will leave the presentation quoting them
  with delight.

- *Resonators* bring ideas to life by pattern-matching them to vivid
  images. These images contain lots of sensory information:
  appeals to sight, sound, touch, taste, smell or feeling. They work
  especially well if they involve human beings doing things. Find
  concrete examples that illustrate your ideas.

- *Attention-grabbers* do just that: they capture or recapture your
  audience's attention. Surprise and suspense work well as
  attention-grabbers. So do figures of speech: turns of phrase or

unusual ways of using language that make ideas stand out memorably. Among the most common figures of speech are metaphor, antithesis (contrast), rhetorical questions and three-part lists.

- *Influencers* give your ideas the weight of authority. You might deliver that authority in your job title, your experience or your behaviour. Information gains credibility if you point out the authority of its source or author. Presenters often try to give their ideas greater influence by quoting famous authors.

- *Stories*, as we've already seen, can be more persuasive than the most authoritative statistics. We believe stories, however fantastical: we identify with the characters and we face their challenges with them. The story of one person can often be more convincing than a mass of carefully documented evidence.

- *Emotions*, as we have already seen, influence us more strongly than reasoned argument. We act on our emotions. Colour your argument with emotion and it will touch parts of the brain that logic cannot reach.

Exercise

Take a Big Idea that you will be arguing for in the near future. On a piece of paper, write down some ideas for examples of each of these PRAISE techniques: proverbial expressions, resonating examples, attention-grabbers, sources of influence, stories and emotional elements.

Designing visuals

'Death by PowerPoint': it's a worryingly familiar phrase. Too many business audiences are now suffering from PowerPoint fatigue. And the overwhelming reason for this fatigue is that presenters are not using slides properly.

Put simply: presenters should be putting *pictures* on slides, not text.

Slides are *visual*. They should offer information that can't be put into words. Why show a visual otherwise? This point is so blazingly obvious that it seems amazing, at first, how many presenters ignore it. But if we look at the way that slide programs have been promoted, the reason for this problem becomes clearer.

Computer slides have been sold to us as a way of making life easier for presenters. We've been told that slides help us prepare and structure our presentation. We've also been told that we can use slides as notes.

We've been seduced, in other words, into putting *text* onto slides, rather than pictures.

In fact, computer-generated slides are the descendants, not of the earlier 35mm slide, but of a much older technology: the blackboard. But – unlike the blackboard – slides display text *before* the speaker speaks it, rather than *while* they speak. The audience is forced to read and listen at the same time – usually, to different text – and they do neither very well (a troubling effect that psychologists call 'cognitive dissonance'). What's more, by flashing a piece of text onto a screen in advance of talking about it, the presenter completely destroys any element of surprise or anticipation.

Slides also flatten the narrative arc of our presentation. As we create one text-heavy slide after another, we lose all sense of increasing tension or crisis in the presentation's structure.

What's worse still, slides seduce presenters into presenting *less well*. They feel forced to 'speak to the slides' (which many do, literally), thus breaking their link with the audience. The presenter is no longer presenting: they have become a voiceover. Result: the audience loses concentration. (Think of what schoolchildren often do when their teacher turns away from them and writes on the blackboard.) Because they are not writing and speaking – as they would with a blackboard – presenters can't decide exactly what to say: should they read out what's on the slide (which is probably too brief and vague to make sense anyway), or paraphrase it (thus increasing the cognitive dissonance for the audience)?

Of course, slides can be effective. But they should *support* your presentation, not substitute for it.

- Remove words. Unless you want to discuss a piece of text, it should not appear on a slide.

- Use pictures. Photos, maps, diagrams – any kind of graphic will do as long as it's *simple* and illustrates a point you're making.

- Create *visual dissonance*. An image on a slide should show less than the audience needs to understand it; you, the presenter, can then resolve the tension by talking about it.

If you *must* put words on slides, make them big enough for the audience to read, and put no more words on the slide than you would expect the audience to read.

Better still: turn off the projector and concentrate on presenting.

Rehearsing

Rehearsal is the reality check. I am astonished at how many presenters think they can simply turn up and run a presentation without rehearsing it. The truth is: you cannot rehearse too much. Rehearsal helps you to remember what you want to say; it helps you to get the timing right; and it helps you to master nerves.

Rehearse success. We so often rehearse failure: we imagine what will go wrong, over and over again. Instead, when you run through your presentation, imagine precisely what you'll do and say – and imagine doing it brilliantly. Imagine speaking confidently and eloquently; imagine the audience listening attentively to your every word and applauding warmly when you have finished.

Rehearse in real time; don't skip bits. Rehearse with a colleague or friend. And rehearse, if you can, at least once in the venue where you'll be presenting.

Rehearsal gives you the freedom to perform when it's time to perform. Once you've rehearsed your material, you'll be better prepared to concentrate on what you should be doing in the presentation itself: talking to the audience.

> **Top tip**
>
> How long should your presentation be? The simple answer is: shorter than you think. Whether you've been told to speak for a certain length of time or not, aim to speak for no more than 20 minutes without a break of some kind. Very few audiences ever wished that a presentation had been longer.

Controlling the audience

Your relationship with the audience matters much, much more than what you say. They will forget most of what you say. But they will remember *you*.

You are performing. Your whole body is involved. You must become aware of what your body is doing so that you can control it, and thus the audience.

Eye contact

We speak more with our eyes than with our voices. Your eyes tell the audience that you're taking notice of them, that you know and *believe* what you are saying.

Use your eyes to control the audience by keeping them under surveillance. Imagine a lighthouse beam shooting out from your eyes and scanning the audience. Make sure that the beam enters every pair of eyes in the room. Focus for a few seconds on each pair of eyes and meet their gaze.

Your face

The rest of your face is important, too! Remember to smile. Animate your face and make everything just a little larger than life so that your face can be 'read' at the back of the room.

Gestures

Find the gestures that are natural for you. If you're a great gesticulator, don't try to force your hands into rigid stillness. If you don't normally gesture a great deal, don't force yourself into balletic movements. Keep your gestures open, away from your body and into the room. Don't cross your hands behind your back, and don't put them in your pockets too much. (It's a good idea to empty your pockets before the presentation so that you don't find yourself jingling coins or keys.)

Movement

Aim for stillness. This does not mean that you should stand completely still all the time. Moving about the room shows that you're making the space your own. But rhythmic, repetitive movement can be annoying and suggest the neurotic pacing of a panther in a cage. Try not to rock on your feet or tie your legs in knots! Aim to have both feet on the ground as much as possible and slow down your movements.

Looking after yourself

And you'll *still* be nervous as the moment of truth approaches. Remember that those nerves are there to help you. If you have prepared adequately, you should be ready to use your nerves to encounter the uncertainty of live performance.

On some occasions, it can be useful to meet the audience and chat with them before you start. This can break the ice and put you more at ease.

Prepare your voice. Along with work on your breathing (we've already discussed 7/11 breathing earlier in this chapter), pay attention to the muscles around your mouth that help you to articulate your words. Try some tongue-twisters or sing a favourite song. Chew the cud, and get your tongue and lips really working and warmed up.

Exercise

A very simple exercise to bring your mouth muscles to life is to stick your tongue as far out of your mouth as you can and then speak a part of your presentation, trying to make the consonants as clear as you can. You only need to do this for about 30 seconds to wake up your voice and make it clearer. You will, of course, look rather silly while doing this, so it's best to do the exercise in a private place!

Answering questions

Many presenters are as worried about the question session as about the presentation itself. A few guidelines can help to turn your question session from a trial into a triumph.

- *Decide when to take questions*. This will probably be at the end. But you might prefer to take questions during the presentation. This is more difficult to manage but can improve your relationship with the audience. Whatever you choose to do, announce your plan to the audience and tell them how you expect them to ask questions.

- *Anticipate the most likely questions*. These may be 'frequently asked questions' that you can easily foresee. Others may arise from the particular circumstances of the presentation.

- *Use a 'plant'*. At the end of a presentation, an audience might hesitate to break the atmosphere by asking the first question. Ask someone to be ready with a question to start the session.

- *Answer concisely*. Force yourself to be brief.

- *Answer honestly.* You can withhold information, but don't lie. Someone in the audience will almost certainly see through you.

- *Take questions from the whole audience.* From all parts of the room and from different 'social areas'.

- *Answer the whole audience.* Don't let questions seduce you into private conversations. Make sure the audience has heard the question.

- *If you don't know, say so.* And promise what you'll do later to answer the question.

Summary points

- To make an effective presentation means taking control of:
  - the material;
  - the audience;
  - yourself.
- To prepare the material:
  - define your objective;
  - analyse your audience;
  - construct a message;
  - create a structure (Monroe's motivated sequence);
  - put it on cards;
  - add spice (PRAISE);
  - design visuals;
  - rehearse.
- To control the audience, work on:
  - eye contact;
  - facial expression;
  - gestures;
  - movement.

- To look after yourself, pay attention to:
  - breathing;
  - articulation;
  - a strategy of answering questions.

08
Putting it in writing

Writing remains one of the most important means of communicating at work. Laura Brown, a consultant and author, surveyed hundreds of business executives over a five-year period from 2016: 89 per cent of her respondents declared that writing still matters a lot. 96 per cent wrote emails regularly, and over half produced reports and proposals.

Laura Brown's survey revealed three key challenges facing business writers:

- 38 per cent told her they felt they needed to write more quickly.
- The same percentage wanted to make their writing 'more compelling'.
- And 36 per cent reported problems making their writing more concise.

Some managers apparently feel so incompetent that they avoid writing completely. That's not surprising: the quality of our writing reflects on us personally. When people judge our writing, they're judging us in our absence. The tone of our writing may give a false impression of the kind of person we are; and, like it or not, our reader won't think well of us if our writing contains mistakes.

The technology of writing is changing rapidly. We read less on paper and more on screen. And most of the time, of course, we aren't actually writing at all; we're *printing*. Screens and computer-generated typefaces create barriers between us and our readers. A paradox: at just the time when social media encourage us to think of writing as a form of conversation, technology is making our writing even less personal.

How, then, can we communicate more effectively through writing? How can we use emails, reports and other documents to generate shared understanding?

Thinking like a reader

Spare a thought for your reader. They're constantly bombarded with written messages: emails (probably more than 120 daily), banner headlines and texts on social media, newsletters, brochures, project updates, thought leadership papers...

Reading is hard work. It consumes a considerable amount of brain power and energy. And, unlike speaking and listening, reading is not a natural activity; it's a skill that we must consciously learn.

So, to write well, we must think like a reader.

Three ways to read like a reader

- **Read your writing aloud**. Is it easy to read? Can you reach the end of a sentence without taking a breath? Do you sound like *you* while you're reading?

- **Take a break before checking your writing**. Allow a little time before sending that email, then read it again. Does everything make sense? Do you need to add anything to help the reader understand you? Can you notice any obvious mistakes?

- **Ask a friend or colleague to read your writing**. Ideally, choose someone who knows as little as possible about what you've written. Tell them to identify anything they don't understand. Ask them to read the text aloud. Where do they hesitate or stumble? Wherever they falter, you can probably find something that you can improve or change.

The three stages of reading

Reading – successful reading, when we don't *notice* that we're reading – happens in (at least) three stages.

First, we must recognize and understand words. This first stage is never as simple as it sounds: many words have multiple meanings; some look and sound similar (*principle* and *principal*, for instance).

At the second stage, sometimes called 'syntactic processing', we allocate meanings to words, based on syntax, which is simply the order of words in a sentence. The sentence *We conducted a survey* gives one meaning to word 'survey' (technically, we recognize it as a noun). The sentence *We survey our members once a year* gives the word 'survey' another meaning (technically, we recognize it as a verb).

At the third stage, sometimes called 'inference-building', we check the meanings we've identified in the text against what we already know – perhaps based on what we have already read – and infer an overall meaning. For instance, look at this sentence.

William realized he would have to break the lock to get free.

If we already know that William is a prisoner – or a kidnap victim – then we can infer that the lock is a metal object, maybe preventing William from opening a door. But if we've been told that William is a wrestler, we would infer that the lock is the hold his opponent has on him, and the meaning of the sentence would be radically different.

The reading contract

Your reader is making a contract with you. They're willing to give pay a certain amount of attention to your text, for a certain amount of time. (Notice that word *pay*: attention is a kind of cost on your reader's brainpower.) The deal they're willing to make with you will depend on the potential benefit of reading your text. Some readers are *browsing*: scrolling through emails on their smartphone, for example, or leafing through a magazine. Their attention span is short and wanders easily. Other readers are *searching*: scrutinizing a detailed report, for example, or studying a white paper. They're willing to pay more attention in the hope of a more substantial return.

In fact, your reader's attention is likely to be shifting along a spectrum between these two poles: browsing and searching. If, while browsing, they find something of interest, they may start to read with closer attention: they'll start searching. And if, while searching, they fail to find the information they're looking for, they'll stop reading and move on: they'll start browsing.

Different kinds of writing tend to sit at different places on the attention spectrum. Email sits at the browsing end, along with leaflets, brochures, information sheets, magazine articles, blog posts and web pages. Reports sit at the searching end, together with minutes of meetings, proposals, research papers, and academic essays.

Online, of course, different tools help us with both types of reading. Browsers help us to move around the internet quickly (and often tempt us with seductive headlines to stop and linger). Search engines help us to find what we're looking for by matching our search terms against text on web pages. Browsers and search engines are essentially attention-management tools.

Your task as a writer is to respond to the contract your reader is making with you. Are they browsing or searching? What do you want them to do as a result of reading? And how can your writing help them do that? Good writing always seeks to address that same question: *What effect am I having on my reader?*

Making reading easier

If your reader starts to find reading difficult, they're likely to do one of three things:

- First, they'll slow down. If you're lucky, they may try to re-read your writing.

- Second, they'll try to extract some meaning from your writing – and, probably, misunderstand it.

- And third, they'll become annoyed and give up.

You won't want your reader to do any of those things. You'll want to make reading as easy as possible. And you can do so in three ways:

- creating useful signposts;

- constructing and sequencing sentences effectively;

- using familiar words.

Using signposts

As your reader scans what you've written, they're looking for clues to help them work out what they're reading. Whatever provides such a clue is a 'signpost'. Actually, we can think of signposts not just as clues, but also as cues: effective signposts help the reader to understand the *context* of your writing.

The most obvious signposts are headings. Carefully written and well placed, headings indicate at a glance what the text is about: they prime the reader for the body text. Better still, develop headings into headlines. Where a heading indicates the subject of the text, a headline tells the reader what you are saying. A heading is like a label on a folder: *Sales Figures in Q3*, for example. A headline – just like a headline in a newspaper – makes a point: for example, *Sales figures increase by 50 per cent in Q3*.

Email subject lines are great places to deliver meaningful headlines. Think of email subject lines as 'message lines'. Put a version of your key message into that line, and the reader will understand what you want to tell them – before they even open the email. In email threads, take care to recast the message in your subject lines so that they continue to align with the content of your email.

In longer documents, develop hierarchies of headings and sub-headings. Together, they can act as an informal outline of your material. They help readers who are searching to find what they're looking for; they can intrigue browsing readers and tempt them to read more.

We can use the same signposting principle in paragraphs. Use the first sentence of a paragraph to summarize what you want to say. This is often called a *topic sentence*. Use the rest of the paragraph to expand on or support that point. In a section made up of paragraphs, the topic sentences should summarize your material. Your reader should be able to read just the topic sentences – in order – and understand a summary of what your text is saying.

You can find good topic sentences in three ways:

- You could write your paragraph first, then find the sentence that summarizes it.

- You could ask what you want to say in the paragraph, write down your topic sentence, and then construct your paragraph to support it.

- Often, you can find a topic sentence by looking at a paragraph's last sentence. Flip that concluding point to the top of the paragraph and see how well it works as a topic sentence.

Exercise

Check out the topic sentences in this book. Take one section of a chapter and read the first sentence of each paragraph in order. Those topic sentences should add up to a summary of the material in that section. If you find a section where topic sentences don't quite work perfectly, see if you can improve what I've written. And please let me know.

As well as helping the reader, signposting helps you as a writer. Signposts help you decide what you want to say. By working on headings, headlines and topic sentences, you can identify the messages and key points that you want to convey.

Holding the reader's attention: using sentences well

Having captured your reader's attention, you need to hold it. And your principal tool for doing that is the sentence. As the copywriter Robert Bruce puts it: 'Every sentence you write should make them want to read the next sentence you write.' Good writers think about how their sentences work, both individually and together. Knowing how sentences work means understanding something about syntax and grammar. (Syntax is the way words are arranged in a sentence. Grammar is the set of principles – some people would say 'rules' – that govern syntax.)

The technical details of sentence construction may be tricky to master, but most of us can recognize a sentence when we see one. A sentence has a capital letter at the beginning, and a full stop at the end.

How to end a sentence (or not...)

There are two alternatives to a full stop: a question mark [?] and an exclamation mark [!]. Use both carefully, and rigorously limit your use of exclamation marks. An unfinished sentence is marked by three dots [...], called ellipsis.

How sentences work

A sentence makes a point. As we read a sentence, we intuitively want to know, as quickly as possible, what point it's making. 'What,' we ask ourselves, 'is this sentence saying?'

A sentence can say something in three ways. (Just for the moment, let's keep things simple.)

- It can make a statement:
  - *Modern consumers care about the environment.*
  - *Our razors have six diamond-coated blades.*
  - *We turn everyday spaces into brighter places.*
- It can ask a question:
  - *Are you looking for the best pushchair money can buy?*
  - *Why should you invest your money with us?*
  - *Installing a new security system in your home?*
- And it can give an instruction or an order:
  - *Discover the turquoise waters and exotic biodiversity of the Seychelles Islands.*
  - *Come to ModelPlanet and have the time of your life!*
  - *Imagine how well you could manage your farm if you had all your data in one place.*

'Characters in a story'

When we read a sentence, we intuitively think of it as telling a story. And, just as with any story, we want to know two things about the sentence as quickly as possible:

- What – or who – is the sentence about?
- And what is it – or they – doing?

The thing or person that the sentence is about is expressed by its *subject*. And what it or they are doing or being is expressed by a *verb*.

The best subjects of sentences act like characters in a story. (Think back to our discussion about stories in Chapter 6.) And the best place to put that character, usually, is at the start of the sentence. If you begin a sentence with a character doing something, your sentence will read more like a miniature story – and your reader will understand it more easily.

A character can be anything you could imagine drawing as a figure in a cartoon. It might be a person: *you, we, customers, the farmer, students*... It might be an organization: *McDonald's, the BBC, Save the Children*... And it might be an object: *the car, the coffee maker, this book*... Phrases like *a recent study*, *my email* or *the attached proposal* can act as a character.

Sometimes, the main character in a sentence isn't obvious. It might be lurking at the end of the sentence – or even in the middle. If you're still uncertain, ask: 'Who is the main character in this sentence?' Put that character at the very start of the sentence and then rebuild the sentence from there.

This sentence, for example, contains no characters.

The decision will be made on Friday.

The effect is formal and rather distant. *The board will make its decision on Friday* introduces a character and the sense of a story. Of course, we could make the style of this sentence even more informal by finding a more powerful verb.

The board will decide on Friday.

Which words to choose?

English has a huge vocabulary. It has grown out of many other languages: French, Latin, and a host of languages from northern Europe and beyond. As a result, English often has two or three words meaning roughly (or *approximately*) the same thing. We can *try* or *endeavour*; we can *start*, *begin* or *commence* doing something; we can *anticipate* or *foresee*.

Different words have different effects. We can place these effects on another spectrum, which we could call 'the style spectrum': formal style at one end, informal (or normal) style at the other. Informal words are the words most often used in speech. Formal words tend to be spoken less frequently; they sound more professional, sophisticated, or academic.

Which are the best words to choose? It depends where you want your writing to sit on the style spectrum. For historical reasons, long words in English will be more formal than short ones. *I anticipate that the project will conclude successfully* is more formally expressed than *I expect the project to end well.*

Many authorities on writing, especially those advocating plain English, advise us to prefer short words to long ones. This advice makes some sense: more people will understand the word *chew* than the word *ruminate*, for example. But sometimes the longer word has a more exact meaning: ruminating, in this example, is a particular kind of chewing. The long word may communicate our meaning more precisely than the shorter one: in technical writing, for example, or if we're writing to a reader whose first language is not English. Prefer the short word to the long word; but don't assume that the shorter word is always the better choice.

Bringing your writing to life

People often tell me: 'I'm not a good writer; I write as I speak. ' In fact, writing as you speak is perhaps one of the best skills to develop as a writer. Good writing does indeed 'speak' to us: we hardly notice that we're reading. We feel that the writer is holding a conversation with us. That's the kind of writing we should be trying to develop.

Bringing your writing to life is a constant challenge. We can build our skills by:

- exploiting the points of maximum attention in our sentences;
- managing sentence length;
- developing our style.

Using the points of maximum attention

Like a good story, every sentence has a beginning, a middle and an end. And, again like a story, the most important points in the sentence are the beginning and the end. As a general rule, as we've seen, place the subject and verb as close to the start of the sentence as possible. The more quickly the reader can find the subject and the main verb, the more easily they will understand the sentence:

> *We [subject] miss [verb] you.*

> *Clients [subject] can rely [verb] on our forty years of experience in this field.*

> *Artificial intelligence [subject] allows [verb] machines to solve complex problems based on what they learn from data.*

But the point of maximum attention, in any sentence, is at the end. (Just as we always want to know what happens at the end of a story.) So, place at the end of the sentence the most important element: maybe the new idea that you want to talk about in the next sentence. In this very simple sentence, for example, the most important word is somewhat lost by being placed in the middle:

> *Life can feel like a whirlwind sometimes.*

If we place that word 'whirlwind' at the end, we give it real power:

> *Sometimes, life can feel like a whirlwind.*

And the reader is primed to read the next sentence (in what ways can life feel like this?)

Using the points of maximum attention – the end-points of sentences – helps us sequence our sentences so that they make more sense. And it helps the reader to move on, to the next sentence.

Managing sentence length

Of course, in order to start reading that next sentence, your reader needs to be able to get to the end of the first sentence easily. Full stops energize your writing: they mark not only the end of a sentence but the beginning of the next one. As sentences get longer and more complicated, they lose energy – and so does your reader.

Follow the '15–25' guideline. Topic sentences and other sentences expressing big ideas should be about 15 words long. No other sentence should exceed 25 words. (As I say, this is a guideline. Some sentences will benefit from being longer, especially if you want to include complex information. Very short sentences can pack a punch.) Simplify sentences that are too complicated; cut long sentences into shorter, well sequenced ones.

Developing your style

While you're writing, imagine speaking to your reader, and write down exactly what you would say to them. You'll find that you naturally adapt your style to the reader you're addressing. Some readers (browsers, in particular) will expect simple, straightforward language; others (searchers, especially) may require a style that is more sophisticated.

Three features in particular affect the quality of our style:

- passive verbs and active verbs;
- abstract nouns;
- unnecessary words.

Passive verbs or active verbs?

Verbs can be either active or passive. An active verb expresses what its subject does; a passive verb expresses what its subject suffers.

The report was written by Sola.

Sola wrote the report.

Sentences with passive verbs will make your writing more formal, and active verbs more informal. In general, prefer active verbs to passive ones; but don't rule out passive verbs. They can help you structure a sentence to emphasize a point differently; they can be useful when you don't know – or don't want to say – who did something. Passive verbs aren't wrong; but active verbs will certainly help to bring your writing to life.

What do you mean, 'abstract nouns'?

Nouns name things, people, times, places or qualities. Concrete nouns name things physically present in the world (*table*, *woman*, *pen*, *car*, *tree*); abstract nouns name ideas, concepts or qualities that cannot be sensed physically (*growth*, *awareness*, *measurement*, *marketing*, *functionality*). Abstract nouns will make your writing more formal. Many abstract nouns are longer words with standard endings: *-ion* (*translation*, *manipulation*, *specification*); *-ment* (*movement*, *management*, *replacement*); *-ence* or *-ance* (*governance*, *maintenance*, *predominance*); or *-ity* (*acidity*, *authority*, *superiority*).

To make your writing more formal, add more abstract nouns. To make your writing less formal, replace abstract nouns with verbs or adjectives. If the only way to replace an abstract noun is to use a group of words, consider keeping it.

Which words do I need?

Some words contribute little to your meaning, but a lot to your tone. *We do these tests every week* says the same thing as *We perform these tests on a weekly basis*, but the second version undoubtedly sounds more professional and impressive. Using words – and adding words – to impress will make your writing more formal. If you remove them, your writing will 'sound' more direct, more 'spoken' – but also, perhaps, less polite. Generally, your writing will improve if it says more with fewer words:

> *The benefits of this arrangement are a saving in consultancy costs and the opportunity for new users to learn the system in a meaningful situation at the same time as they learn their jobs.*

> *This arrangement saves consultancy costs and allows new users to learn the system as part of on-the-job learning.*

Exercise

Pick an email that you wrote some time ago. Rewrite it, choosing to shift its style towards one or other end of the style spectrum. Try to say exactly the same thing as in the original; try not to alter the meaning. What do you notice about the rewrites? How do you think the reader would react to your new version?

Summary points

- To develop your writing skills, begin by thinking like a reader:
  - read your writing aloud;
  - take a break before checking your writing;
  - ask a friend or colleague to read your writing.
- Reading happens in (at least) three stages:
  - First, we must recognize and understand words.
  - At the second stage, often known as 'syntactic processing', we allocate meanings to words based on syntax, which is simply the order of words in a sentence.
  - At the third stage, sometimes called 'inference-building', we check the meanings we've identified in the text against what we already know.
- Your reader is making a contract with your writing. They may be *browsing* or *searching*.
  And their attention is likely to be moving between these two activities.
  We can make reading easier by:

- creating useful signposts;

- constructing and sequencing sentences effectively;

- using familiar words.

- Signposts can be headings, headlines, or topic sentences of paragraphs.

  A sentence always makes a point. Make your sentences easier to understand by making the subject act like a character in a story, and then by making the verb express what the character is doing in the story.

  Think about which words to choose, especially choosing between long and short words.

  We can bring our writing to life, in part, by:

- exploiting the points of maximum attention in our sentences;

- managing sentence length;

- developing our style.

- The point of maximum attention in a sentence is at the end. Place at the end of your sentences words you want to emphasize or go on to talk about.

  Follow the '15–25' guideline in sentence length.

  Develop your style, in part, by looking at:

- passive verbs and active verbs;

- abstract nouns;

- unnecessary words.

09
Tough conversations

At some point in your career, you'll have to hold a tough conversation. It goes, as they say, with the territory. Any book about improving your communication skills should help you with the conversations you struggle with. (Of course, we also have to hold tough conversations outside work. This book focuses on communication in the workplace, but the skills we discuss are applicable in personal conversations too.)

To misquote Tolstoy: all happy conversations are alike; all tough conversations are tough in their own way. When conversations go well, it's usually for similar reasons: rapport is high, we're talking the same language, and the conversation's objective is clear. In contrast, conversations can become tough for different reasons. Some are predictable; many take us completely by surprise.

Six tough conversations

Holly Weeks sets out six broad types of tough conversation in her book, *Failure to Communicate*. You'll probably recognize all six.

- *I've got bad news.* Every manager, at some point, will need to tell someone something they don't want to hear.

- *You're challenging my power.* The opposite, in some ways, of the previous conversation: you need to raise a problem with your manager, and you're worried that they may feel threatened.

- *I can't go there.* If you are conflict-averse, you may try to avoid the tough conversation – and make it tougher.

- *You win/I lose.* You're trying to be cooperative and the other person insists on making it competitive – and trying to win.

- *What's going on here?* A calm conversation suddenly becomes charged with negative emotion. Perhaps an innocent remark has been taken entirely the wrong way, with catastrophic consequences.

- *I'm being attacked.* The other person in the conversation suddenly starts accusing, shouting, threatening or being abusive.

What makes conversations tough?

Difficult conversations become tough when they develop three features. First, we sense – sometimes suddenly, shockingly – that we don't understand what's going on. In particular, we have no idea why the other person is behaving as they are. Second, emotion rears its head, clouding our judgement and dictating all sorts of unhelpful tactics. Among those tactics is the third key feature of a tough conversation: conflict.

Each of these three elements can cause us to make the conversation tougher.

The fog of uncertainty

A conversation becomes tough when we can't see what's happening. In particular, we find it impossible to read the other person's intentions. As a result, we make assumptions about those intentions – and those assumptions tend to take a predictable form. All too often, we allocate blame.

Blame is, in fact, a completely natural and understandable reaction to uncertainty. It grows out of that preference for cause-and-effect explanations that we explored in Chapter 6. Faced with a situation that we don't understand, we will tend to assume that it's been created by someone – or something – *deliberately*. We might blame the gods for natural catastrophes; we construct conspiracy theories to explain extraordinary tragedies. We blame, even when there's no one obvious to blame: we shout at the computer when it crashes, we kick a burst tyre. In a conversation, blame is a natural response to behaviour we can't read clearly.

Top tip

If you finding yourself blaming someone, try one or more of these tactics. Stop generalizing. What makes this situation different? Resist the temptation to make life difficult for the person. Separate the problem from the person. Talk to them about it.

As well as finding it impossible to read the other person's intentions, we find it hard to read their reactions to what we are saying. Mostly, we can exercise what psychologists call a theory of mind: we can infer the other person's thoughts and feelings by reading their behaviour. In a tough conversation, the readings we pick up from their gestures, facial expressions and verbal responses fail to add up: they're confusing or contradictory. Something is not quite right, but we can't work out what it is.

Emotional arousal

Faced with these uncertainties, our minds tend to respond emotionally.

Think of your brain as being like an office building with three floors. (This explanation of brain function – it's called the *triune brain* – is grossly simplified but nonetheless helpful.) In the basement (usually called the brain stem) are the control systems for the body's vital functions: heart rate, breathing, body temperature, balance and so on. On the ground floor – it's actually in the centre of the brain – is the limbic system, which acts as a kind of reception area for all the information that enters the brain. Sitting at the front desk in the limbic system is the amygdala, which we can think of as a kind of security officer. The amygdala has a very simple job: it pattern-matches incoming information and gives it a visitor's badge, in the form of an emotional tag. If the visitor is welcome, the amygdala sends it up to the top floor of the brain, the neocortex, which can think more subtly and intelligently about the information.

But if the amygdala decides that the information is unwelcome, it will tag it as dangerous. It's like a security alert. And the first thing that happens in a security alert, of course, is that the lifts are closed down. No more shuttling between floors; no more subtle, intelligent thinking. The limbic system cuts off all neural connections to the neocortex and calls in the emotions to deal with the threat. We call this *emotional arousal*: in the words of Daniel Goleman, author of *Emotional Intelligence*, the limbic system hijacks the neocortex. It's a survival mechanism, helping us to deal with a situation *without needing to think about it*.

The problem, of course, is that this emotional arousal only serves to make a tough conversation tougher. The emotions – the fear, anger or embarrassment – are telling us to act: to do something *now*, without stopping to think. The limbic system has reduced our options to just two: run away, or fight it out. Hence the name: the *fight-or-flight response*.

The combat mentality

If one person in a conversation is experiencing the fight-or-flight response, the conversation is likely to become difficult. The other person may have to use all their skill to reduce their emotional arousal and cancel the security alert in their brain. But all too often, faced with aggressive behaviour, our own limbic systems respond to the threat – and what Holly Weeks calls the combat mentality is established.

The combat mentality treats the conversation as a battle. Every move is seen as an unprovoked attack, and the only strategy available to our brains – locked down in that limbic security alert – is to defend or attack. The combat mentality can cause real damage: bruising emotional wounds that can leave permanent scars on a working relationship.

How we make tough conversations tougher

These three elements – uncertainty, emotional arousal, the combat mentality – act together. Between them, they create a self-reinforcing, vicious cycle. As it spirals out of control, we feel increasingly powerless to intervene. We may want to save the conversation; we may even be able to see what's going wrong. But we can't think about what to do. Instead, the cycle dictates our behaviour.

First, as we've seen, we blame the other person for the problem. And in blaming them, we assume ourselves to be innocent. That assumption of innocence can become what Holly Weeks calls 'the delusion of good intentions': the idea that tough conversations shouldn't happen to us, because we mean well and we always try to do our best. It's a delusion because it doesn't take account of how we might be contributing to the other person's behaviour. As a result, we evade responsibility for the conversation. We justify what we do as the inevitable result of what *they* are doing, and *only* what they are doing.

Second, emotional arousal leads us to oversimplify the problem. Simplifying our thinking is one of the prime functions of emotions: they make it easier for us to choose what to do. In fact, we *don't* choose what to do; the emotion chooses for us.

Our resulting strategies respond to the oversimplified problem by forcing an oversimplified solution. The emotions force us into black-and-white thinking: this or that, good or bad. We might try to force through an either/or decision: yes or no, your way or my way, take it or leave it. Or we might go for the generalizing strategy:

this is *always* what happens when we discuss this issue, it's *always* bad, and this is what we *always* do to deal with it.

And third, the combat mentality dictates a whole host of strategies. Battles have only two outcomes: win or lose. Once we've taken on the combat mentality, every move must aim to win. For example, we might notice the other person engaging in what Holly Weeks calls 'thwarting ploys'. The aim of these ploys, she writes, 'is to get us to back off, to make our counterparts themselves come out on top, or to get out of the conversation altogether'.

Thwarting ploys come in all shapes and sizes. Some are defensive, some offensive; some manage to be both. They might include:

- bursting into tears;
- laughing off a derogatory remark as a joke;
- pleading external duties that make it impossible to stop and talk;
- switching the topic of conversation unexpectedly.

The most successful thwarting ploys have one feature in common: they're hard to read. We've come full circle, back to that first key feature of tough conversations: the fog of uncertainty. Thwarting ploys add to the uncertainty for the other person; that's why we use them. What's worse, when we spot a thwarting ploy, we often assume that we know why the other person is using it. But of course, we might be wrong. Is the other person wilfully, or genuinely, mis-understanding what we say? Are they evading the issue or simply changing the subject? Are they upset or putting it on?

Three steps towards better tough conversations

How can we break this cycle? Given the complexity of tough conversations – the fog of uncertainty, the swirl of emotion, the smoke of combat – can we find tactics that are simple enough to remember and practise?

Holly Weeks suggests that our strategy should begin with three-way respect. We should respect ourselves, the other person and the conversation itself.

Self-respect, to begin with, means paying attention to our own needs.

What humans need

We all have needs that we must meet in order to function as effective human beings. Some needs are physical; others are psychological.

Physical Needs	Psychological Needs
Air	Security
Water	Attention
Nutritious food	A sense of autonomy and control
Sleep	Emotional connections to others
Sensory stimulation	Membership of a community
Physical exercise	Friendship, fun, love, intimacy
Shelter	Sense of status in social situations
Safety	Sense of competence and achievement
	Meaning and purpose:
	– people who need us
	– activities that stretch us (flow; peak experiences that focus our attention; being 'in the zone')
	– connection to a bigger picture

A conversation can become tough if one of us feels that something in the conversation threatens a need. If you sense resistance – either in yourself or in the other person – ask yourself, 'What need is being threatened here?'

This model of human needs is based on the Human Givens approach, pioneered by Joe Griffin and Ivan Tyrrell.

Self-respect means meeting our needs. Among the most important of those needs are:

- Competence: the sense that we're good at what we do.

- Autonomy: the sense that we're in control of our lives.

- Relatedness: the sense that we're connected to others.

(The mnemonic 'CAR' will help you to remember these three core needs.) Meeting our needs doesn't mean ignoring the needs of others. Neither does it mean using thwarting ploys to protect our need. A ploy is likely to protect us only in the short term; self-respect means knowing that we need to meet our needs more fully and deeply.

Respect for the other person means acknowledging that they, too, have the same needs that we have. Respecting them doesn't mean that we must agree with them or give way to them. Neither does it mean that we should like them. It means simply that we should recognize that they have needs and interests of their own.

Of course, part of what they're doing is responding to what *we* are saying and doing. It may be extremely important to them, for example, not to lose face: not to be embarrassed or humiliated publicly. So respecting the other person also means seeking to understand how our behaviour might be affecting their self-esteem. (*What effect am I having?*) This means understanding our own behaviour more deeply. Thus, respect for ourselves and for the other person reinforce each other.

Finally, respecting the conversation means recognizing it for what it is: tough. Holly Weeks suggests that we view a tough conversation as a landscape to be navigated. 'Rather than put our heads down and start to plough through,' she writes, 'we will do better to step back, take a satellite view and think about the lay of the land.' We're looking for an effective route through the obstacles that this conversation is likely to throw up.

How does this three-way respect play out in practice? What can we *do*?

We could start by considering the context of the conversation. Do you need to act on either of these questions?

- *Time.* Is this the right time? What is the history behind the conversation?

- *Place.* Are you somewhere comfortable, quiet, and – perhaps above all – private?

If you pick the right time and the right place, the conversation has a better chance of turning out better. And there are other tactics we could choose to try.

But we do need to *choose* what to do. A tough conversation is unlikely to improve by chance. The three elements – the fog of uncertainty, emotional arousal and the combat mentality – act as a mutually reinforcing cycle. We can start anywhere in the cycle. But we need to start somewhere. And only *we* can choose to act. We can't predict what the other person does, and we may not be able to control their behaviour directly. But we can influence their behaviour by what we do. It's up to us.

Clearing the fog of uncertainty

If we want to reduce uncertainty in a tough conversation, we need more information. We need to use all the skills of enquiry that we can muster.

A good first step is to banish blame. As we have seen, blame encourages us to believe that the other person's intentions are hostile towards us. If we simply reverse this assumption, we open up new possibilities for gaining information.

The principle is: *assume constructive intent.* (We've mentioned this tactic before, at the end of Chapter 4.) Assume that the other person is doing what they're doing, and saying what they're saying, for good reasons: reasons that make sense to them. They are trying to meet their needs for competence, autonomy or relatedness, in some way. Assume, also, that they may not *know* precisely why they're doing what they're doing.

It is possible, even in the threatening confusion of a tough conversation, to make this very simple move. But assuming constructive intent will be easier if you've practised the skill beforehand.

Exercise
Assuming constructive intent

Try this whenever you are relaxed and able to observe someone's behaviour without feeling threatened by it. (Meetings are good opportunities to do this exercise. You might be observing two people discussing an issue, without participating directly yourself.) The moment to watch for is when someone disagrees with a remark or seems to show resistance. Ask yourself the question: 'What good reason might they have for resisting or disagreeing?' Test your thinking using the three needs we have mentioned: competence, autonomy, relatedness. Is it possible that one of these needs is being threatened? How could you find out, if you were taking part in this conversation?

The next move is to ask questions. A really powerful information-gathering tool is the ladder of inference. Look back at Chapter 3: you'll find plenty of questions there that will help you to climb down the ladder of inference and explore the beliefs and facts underlying what the other person is saying.

We often go into conversations knowing that they will be difficult. In those cases, we can plan the questioning strategy to help us clear the fog of uncertainty. The trick is to have lots of questions ready, and be ready to change direction at any point. Plan, but don't script.

Reducing emotional arousal

That tangled thicket of emotions is probably the greatest obstacle in your path through a tough conversation. Although we're looking at emotions as the second element of tough conversations, you may need to tackle emotional arousal first, before you can make any more progress.

Why can emotions be so disabling? Because they stop us thinking clearly. That's their natural function (and this bears repeating): emotions tell us how to act *without thinking*. (Look back at the notes on *pathos* in Chapter 5. E-*motions* provoke *motion*.) Tough conversations, more than any others, need us to think clearly. Extreme, negative emotions get in the way of clear thinking.

How can we reduce emotional arousal? Work on yourself before trying to influence the other person. The first step is to focus on your breathing. Take a couple of deep breaths and try to breathe *out* for longer than you breathe *in*. This technique is called 7/11 *breathing*.

Top tip

You can find an exercise to help you do 7/11 breathing in Chapter 7.

You should have plenty of time to work on your breathing while listening to the other person answering your questions; if you can't seem to find the space to breathe for a moment, you may be talking too much!

Now slow the conversation down. Review the material in Chapter 3 on managing time. A very effective way to slow the pace of the conversation is to work on your voice: lower the volume, lower the pitch and lower the pace. The effect on the other person can be magical: it's very hard to counter the effect of a soothing voice. But you must practise the technique so that you can engage it when you need to; the emotion of a tough conversation will be working hard against you.

You can alter your breathing and your voice in a matter of seconds. Now focus on the words of the conversation. If you repeat and paraphrase what the other person has been saying, you will discharge some of the emotion.

For example, if the other person says 'The sales targets are just too high', you could paraphrase by saying: 'So let me get this right. Are you saying that the sales targets have been *set* too high?' The paraphrase – especially if posed as a question – gives the other person the opportunity to reflect on their thinking, develop it or examine it. Paraphrasing can help both of you to think more objectively about the problem.

Paraphrasing can also slow down a conversation and instil a little calm – a tough conversation is unlikely to become relaxed, but at least you'll now have the chance to navigate it more successfully.

From conflict to collaboration

Collaboration means working together to navigate the landscape of the conversation. One way to do that is to take a 'satellite view' of the conversation's subject.

Try running a 'how to' exercise. The technique is almost ridiculously simple: we define the problem as a phrase beginning with the words 'how to'. Invite the other person to join you in creating a 'how to' statement that defines the problem you are discussing. Offer your own 'how to' if you wish, and spend some time generating new, alternative 'how to' statements: different ways of defining the problem, different views of the problem, parts of the problem. Questions that will help you to generate more 'how to' statements include:

- What are we trying to achieve here?
- What do you want to do?
- If we could do this, what other problem would that solve?
- What do we need to do in order to do this?

Top tip

Writing down the 'how to' statements will help you to objectify the problem still further. Sticky notes are useful: write each 'how to' on a separate note and start clustering them. By visualizing the problem in this way, you give yourself a greater opportunity to collaborate on solving it.

'How to' is a powerful first-stage thinking technique. (Look back at the section on structuring your thinking in Chapter 3.) It works particularly well as part of the second conversation in the sequence of four that we explored in Chapter 3: the conversation for possibility.

Edward de Bono, as we have seen in Chapter 3, calls conflict 'adversarial thinking'. According to de Bono, there are four main types of adversarial thinking.

- Critical thinking: looking for what is wrong with an idea.

- Ego thinking: identifying ourselves with our idea, so that attacking the idea becomes a personal attack.

- Political thinking: using ideas to create allies or destroy alliances.

- Rigid thinking: simplifying and reducing complexity so that ideas become impossible to develop or change.

You may be able to detect one or more of these types of thinking in the tough conversation you're holding. If so, these questions may help to defuse conflict and increase the chances of collaboration.

- To counter critical thinking, ask: 'What is good about this idea?'

- To counter ego thinking, ask: 'When does this happen? In what circumstances does this idea *not* apply?'

- To counter political thinking, ask: 'What are the strengths and weaknesses of this idea?'

- To counter rigid thinking, ask: 'What if…? What if… happened? What if… were not happening? What if… you could solve this problem?'

Tough conversations demand more than good intentions. They demand clear thinking, a clear strategy and clear tactics. Navigating a tough conversation doesn't mean ignoring the needs of the other person, but neither does it mean giving way or running away. We may not be able to understand or influence the other person's behaviour in a tough conversation – that's part of what makes it tough – but we *can* alter our own behaviour. The techniques we've explored in this chapter help us to improve the prospects for a tough conversation by acting on our side.

These techniques have one thing in common. We need to practise them before we need to use them. We can try out most of them in relaxed conversations. Once we understand how they can help us, we will be ready whenever a conversation becomes tough.

Summary points

- Tough conversations have three key features:
  - the fog of uncertainty, particularly in reading the other person's intentions;
  - emotional arousal;
  - a combat mentality.
- We can make tough conversations tougher by making poor tactical choices:
  - The fog of uncertainty encourages us to blame the other person for the problem, and creates a delusion of good intentions.
  - Emotional arousal causes us to oversimplify the problem and seek oversimplified solutions: forced either/or decisions, or generalized judgements.

- The combat mentality provokes many strategies, including thwarting ploys.

- We can only manage tough conversations better if we respect ourselves, the other person and the conversation itself:

  - Self-respect means understanding our own needs and working to meet them.

  - Respecting the other person means remembering their needs and that they are trying to meet them.

  - Respecting the conversation means thinking about it as a landscape to be navigated together.

- We can adopt a number of techniques to break the cycle of a tough conversation:

  - We can clear the fog of uncertainty by assuming constructive intent, asking questions and using the ladder of inference.

  - We can reduce emotional arousal by working on our breathing and our voice, and by paraphrasing the other person's remarks before responding to them.

  - We can transform combat into collaboration by using the 'how to' technique, and by responding carefully to the four forms of adversarial thinking: critical thinking, ego thinking, political thinking and rigid thinking.

- Tough conversations demand more than good intentions. They demand clear thinking, a clear strategy and clear tactics. We need to practise these techniques before finding ourselves in a tough conversation.

APPENDIX
Where to go from here

Communication is continuous, and we never finish learning how to improve. My blog explores issues and events relating to the material in this book. You can find it at: bit.ly/1zgJBvo (archived at https://perma.cc/75TS-QEG9).

Here are some thoughts about books and other resources that will take further the ideas we've explored in this book.

About this book

You can find a copy of the Economist Intelligence Unit's report, *Communication Barriers in the Modern Workplace*, here: https://bit.ly/2OTJ2Vn (archived at https://perma.cc/WEH7-NEJM).

Find a link to the Interact consultancy's report here: https://bit.ly/2DhDrmF (archived at https://perma.cc/Y664-YQTN).

The GMAC's 2017 Corporate Recruiters Survey is available here: https://bit.ly/2Pwo5Au (archived at https://perma.cc/N6PZ-SY26).

Chapter 1: What is communication?

The fullest explanation I have found of the transmission model of communication is on Mick Underwood's magnificent (and award-winning) website: bit.ly/29CaP7Q (archived at https://perma.cc/W8AT-YNJ4).

I draw on the work of Joe Griffin and Ivan Tyrrell throughout this book. You can find out about their work by going to the Human Givens Institute website (hgi.org.uk (archived at https://perma.cc/XAP7-AXZH)). Their book, *Human Givens: The new approach to emotional health and clear thinking*, is an excellent introduction to this body of knowledge and research.

Chris Dyas explains his five steps to building rapport here: bit.ly/29xhu5U (archived at https://perma.cc/D7NJ-TA96).

The Wikipedia article on Paul Watzlawick provides useful information and links.

Chapter 2: What's your communication style?

My model of communication styles draws on a number of sources. I've borrowed the term 'functional' from the styles model illustrated in the 2017 report by the Economist Intelligence Unit. This model seems to be based on the work of Mark Murphy, founder of Intelligence IQ – although the report does not, I think, acknowledge him. Murphy's model is broadly similar to the Wilson Social Styles model and the Insights Discovery method, both of which I have used in my own consultancy work. You can find information on all three approaches online. Insights claims that the Discovery product, like the Myers-Briggs profile, is a personality assessment tool, drawing on the work of Carl Gustav Jung. My own model doesn't claim to demonstrate anything about personality.

The 'push' and 'pull' influencing styles are part of situational influencing theory, often associated with the work of David Berlew and Roger Harrison.

Empathizing and systemizing are concepts used by Simon Baron-Cohen. Check out his book, *The Essential Difference*, for more information (Penguin, London, 2003).

Chapter 3: Seven ways to improve your conversations

First- and second-stage thinking are notions that inform Edward de Bono's work. Look at *Lateral Thinking in Management* (Penguin, London, 1982). The four types of conversation derive from the work of Michael Wallacek, who may have been influenced by Werner Erhard.

Chris Argyris's ladder of inference is best found in *The Fifth Discipline Fieldbook*, edited by Peter Senge and others (Nicholas Brealey, London, 1994).

For more on mind maps, see Tony Buzan's *Use your Head* (BBC, London, 1974).

Chapter 4: The skills of enquiry

Nancy Kline's *Time to Think* (Ward Lock, London, 1999) is a fascinating study of deep listening.

Chapter 5: The skills of persuasion

Aristotle explains his three modes of appeal in *The Art of Rhetoric* (Penguin Classics, London, 1991).

Caroline Goyder includes her ideas on voice production in her book *Gravitas* (Vermilion, London, 2014).

Jay Heinrichs talks about the tenses of persuasion in his book *Thank You for Arguing* (Three Rivers Press, New York, 2013).

Peter Thompson's *Persuading Aristotle* (Kogan Page, London, 1999) entertainingly relates classical rhetoric to modern business techniques.

For more on pyramids, look at Barbara Minto's *The Pyramid Principle* (Pitman, London, 1987).

Chapter 6: Storytelling and the uses of narrative

This article is a good academic introduction to storytelling and includes an extensive reading list: Bietti, Lucas M, Tilston, O, Banderter, A (2018) *Storytelling as Adaptive Collective Sense-making*. Topics in cognitive science, Wiley Online Library. https://doi.org/10.1111/tops.12358 (archived at https://perma.cc/T8KW-3H3Z).

Robin Dunbar makes a persuasive case for the evolutionary development of storytelling in this paper: Dunbar, R I M. 2014. *How conversations around campfires came to be*. Proceedings of the National Academy of Sciences. https://doi.org/10.1073/pnas.1416382111 (archived at https://perma.cc/NGU6-VAZ7).

I've also been strongly influenced by his ideas in *Grooming, Gossip and the Evolution of Language*, Faber and Faber, London, 2004.

Randy Olson applies narrative to science communication in *Houston, We Have a Narrative* (University of Chicago Press, 2015). His ideas are eminently transferable to business and corporate storytelling, particularly for technical specialists and researchers.

Chapter 7: Making a presentation

You can find a worked example of Monroe's motivated sequence here: bit.ly/1ndUE4m (archived at https://perma.cc/F6Z8-CEQV).

PRAISE is based loosely on the material in *Made to Stick* by Chip and Dan Heath (Arrow, London, 2008).

Jens Kjeldsen has analysed slide usage in his paper, 'The Rhetoric of PowerPoint': bit.ly/2O9vX7d (archived at https://perma.cc/M6N9-ZAHJ).

Max Atkinson's book *Lend Me Your Ears* (Vermilion, London, 2004) takes a strikingly new approach to the subject of presenting and speech writing.

Chapter 8: Putting it in writing

Some of the best practical advice on writing has come from the University of Chicago. I refer regularly to *Style* by Joseph M Williams and Joseph Bizup (Pearson, 12th edition, London, 2016). I'm also a fan of Helen Sword: *The Writer's Diet* (University of Chicago Press, 2nd edition, 2016). William Germano's *Revision: The Only Writing That Counts* (University of Chicago Press, 2020) is one of the latest in a long line of distinguished titles from this publisher.

Check out online lectures on YouTube – again from the University of Chicago – by Larry McEnerney: *The Craft of Writing Effectively* and *Writing Beyond the Academy*.

Joe Moran provides excellent reflections on how to write well in *First You Write a Sentence* (Penguin, London, 2019).

MaryAnne Wolf explores the science of reading in *Proust and the Squid* (Icon Books, Cambridge, 2008).

David Crystal's *Making Sense: The Glamorous Story of English Grammar* (Profile Books, London, 2017) is a great introduction to some of the technicalities of writing.

Alan Barker's *Writing at Work* (Industrial Society, London, 1999) is a comprehensive guide to writing business documents.

Chapter 9: Tough conversations

Find out how well Paul McLean's model of the triune brain is surviving:

bit.ly/1PaQK8G (archived at https://perma.cc/6ABL-NB74).

bit.ly/1PB8vID (archived at https://perma.cc/SVL3-FFJU).

Find out more about the limbic system here: bit.ly/29HkLz9 (archived at https://perma.cc/955K-6XF6).

Explore our needs as human beings here: bit.ly/29xg4mm (archived at https://perma.cc/WC92-8Q62).

And you can take an online emotional needs audit here: bit.ly/29xg1at (archived at https://perma.cc/M35K-NUFG).

All the books in the Creating Success series